THE DAY PEARL HARBOR WAS BOMBED

A Photo History of World War II

by George Sullivan

SCHOLASTIC INC.
New York   Toronto   London   Auckland   Sydney

Cover Photos

Top photo: December 7, 1941, the battleship *Arizona*, stationed at Pearl Harbor, burns out of control (USS *Arizona* Photographic Collection).

Bottom photos, clockwise from top left: A formation of British Lancasters (National Archives); December 8, 1941, President Roosevelt signs the declaration of war against Japan (F.D.R. Library, Hyde Park, New York); American soldiers in the South Pacific (Press Association, Inc.); Hitler, mapping strategy with his generals (National Archives); Fires rage out of control in bombed, blacked-out London (Smithsonian Institution, National Air and Space Museum); Victorious American soldiers raise the flag at Iwo Jima, 1945 (AP/Wide World).

Back cover: December 7, 1941, burning and damaged ships at Pearl Harbor (National Archives).

Interior Photo Credits

Pages 5 and 47: U.S. Navy. Page 6: USS *Arizona* Photographic Collection. Pages 7, 59, 66, 68, 84, and 87: *The New York Times*. Pages 8, 9, 12, 13, 14 (bottom), 15 (left), 16 (left), 17, 19, 20, 23, 27, 30, 32 (inset), 33, 34, 35, 36, 39, 40, 41, 42 (right), 45, 46, 48, 50, 51 (left), 54 (larger photo by Dorothea Lange), 58, 62, 63 (inset), 69, 70 (inset), 72, 73, 74 (left), 75, 77, 78, 79, 80, and 83: National Archives. Pages 9 (inset) and 29 (inset): George Sullivan. Pages 10 (left), 29, and 90: The Franklin D. Roosevelt Library. Pages 10 (right) and 11 (left): U.S. Army. Pages 11 (right), 25 (top), 26, 32, 35 (inset), 43 (inset), 49 (bottom), 55, 64, 65, 67, 70, 76, 81, and 88: AP/Wide World. Pages 14 (top) and 21: Ed Stadnicki. Page 15 (right): Tom Veres. Pages 16 (right), 28, and 53 (left): Queens Borough Public Library; New York *Herald Tribune* Collection. Pages 18, 25 (middle), 31, 43, 56, 60, and 85: UPI/Bettmann. Page 21 (inset): Herb Field Art Studio. Pages 22, 23 (inset), and 52: Smithsonian Institution; National Air and Space Museum. Page 24: British Combine. Page 37: U.S. Air and Space Museum. Pages 38 and 74 (right): Defense Department Photo (Marine Corps). Page 42 (left): Sovfoto. Pages 44, 57, 63, and 71: Dwight D. Eisenhower Library. Page 49 (top): U.S. Army Air Force. Page 51 (right): Smithsonian Institution. Page 53 (right): Herman Darvick. Page 58 (inset): Sy Kessler. Page 60 (inset): Harris and Ewing. Page 61: Signal Corps. Page 81 (inset): The White House. Page 82: U.S. Air Force. Page 88 (inset): Harry S Truman Library. Page 86: Army News Features. Page 91: The United Nations.

Acknowledgments

Many people helped the author in providing background information and photographs for use in this book. Special thanks are due the following: Dale Connolly, National Archives and Records Administration; Larry Wilson, Dave Spencer, Smithsonian Institution, National Air and Space Museum; Benedict Zobrist, Harry S Truman Library; Susan Elter, P. M. McLaughlin, Franklin D. Roosevelt Library; Martin Teasley, Dwight D. Eisenhower Library; Russel D. Egnor, Department of the Navy; Charles Young, Director, and William Asadorian, Archivist, Long Island Division, Queens Borough Public Library; Blanca Stransky, USS *Arizona* Memorial; Franca Kurti; TLC Custom Labs; Herman Darvick; Ed Stadnicki; Sy Kessler; and Tim Sullivan.

Book design by David Tommasino

ISBN 0-590-43449-7

Copyright © 1991 by George Sullivan.
All rights reserved. Published by Scholastic Inc.

12 11 10 9 8 7 6   3 4 5 6/9

Printed in the U.S.A.   34

First Scholastic printing, December 1991

TABLE OF CONTENTS

"Real Planes, Real Bombs; This Is No Drill!" 5
America Goes to War 10
Aggression on the March 12
Blitzkrieg! 16
Retreat to Dunkirk 18
The Fall of France 20
The Battle of Britain 22
Hitler Invades Russia 26
The United States: Arsenal of Democracy 28
Japan's Pacific Conquests 30
America Strikes Back 33
Guadalcanal 38
The U-boat Threat 40
The Battle of Stalingrad 42
"Operation Torch" 44
The Invasion of Italy 46
The Air War to Cripple German Industries 50
On the Home Front 52
D-Day 57
The Battle of the Bulge 62
Germany Surrenders 64
The Holocaust 69
Winning in the Pacific 72
Return to the Philippines 75
Attacking Japan by Air and Sea 79
Iwo Jima and Okinawa 80
The Atomic Bomb 82
Victory 86
Keeping the Peace 90
Memorable Dates, 1933–1946 92
For Further Reading 93
Index 94

An aerial view of Pearl Harbor taken several weeks before the attack. Battleships are anchored in pairs between Ford Island (center) and the mainland.

Japanese bombers warm up on the flight deck of the carrier _Kiryu_ before the attack.

"Real Planes, Real Bombs; This Is No Drill!"

The sun was bright and warm on the lazy Sunday morning when Pearl Harbor was bombed. High white clouds drifted in the Hawaiian sky. December 7, 1941, was a perfect day.

Around Ford Island in the middle of the harbor, lay the ships of the U.S. Pacific Fleet — veteran cruisers and clusters of sleek destroyers, small repair and supply vessels and, on the far side of the island, anchored in pairs, several big and powerful battleships, the pride of the fleet.

At Wheeler Field, the army air base in the center of Oahu Island, more than 60 new P-40 fighters were lined up carefully on the concrete runways. The Army's bombers were based at Hickam Field, closer to Honolulu. Like the fighters, the bombing planes were all arranged in neat rows.

After being ripped apart by an explosion, the battleship <u>Arizona</u> burns out of control.

It was a typical Sunday morning at the home of the Pacific Fleet. On every ship, men were still at breakfast. Some lazed about on open decks. Those off duty for the day were preparing to go ashore. The Marines aboard the cruiser *Helena* were getting ready for a softball game.

A number of men were thinking about Christmas. Only 15 shopping days were left. Aboard the battleship *Maryland*, a sailor wrote out Christmas cards.

On the battleship *Nevada*, the ship's band assembled for the raising of the flag, a traditional ceremony held each morning when the vessel was in port. As the band members took their places, some of them noticed specks on the sky. Planes were approaching.

The officer of the deck on the cruiser *Raleigh* saw a line of planes coming in

"All the News That's Fit to Print."

The New York Times.

LATE CITY EDITION
Increasing cloudiness with rising temperature today. Tomorrow cloudy, somewhat colder.
Temperatures Yesterday—Max.,34; Min.,25

Copyright, 1941, by The New York Times Company.

VOL. XCI No. 30,634. Entered as Second-Class Matter, Postoffice, New York, N. Y. NEW YORK, MONDAY, DECEMBER 8, 1941. THREE CENTS NEW YORK CITY and Vicinity

JAPAN WARS ON U. S. AND BRITAIN; MAKES SUDDEN ATTACK ON HAWAII; HEAVY FIGHTING AT SEA REPORTED

CONGRESS DECIDED

Roosevelt Will Address It Today and Find It Ready to Vote War

CONFERENCE IS HELD

Legislative Leaders and Cabinet in Sober White House Talk

By C. P. TRUSSELL
Special to THE NEW YORK TIMES.

WASHINGTON, Dec. 7—President Roosevelt will address a joint session of Congress tomorrow and will find the membership in a mood to vote any steps he asks in connection with the developments in the Pacific.

The President will appear personally at 12:30 P. M. Whether he would call for a flat declaration of war again Japan was left unannounced tonight. But leaders of Congress, shocked and angered by the Japanese attacks, were talking of a declaration of war on not only Japan but on the entire Axis.

The plans for action tomorrow were made tonight in a White House conference at which the President, surrounded by his Cabinet and by Congressional leaders of both parties, went through reports, some official, some unconfirmed, of the continued assaults of the Japanese upon American Pacific outposts.

Meet Far Into Night

The conference lasted until after 11 o'clock and at its close an official statement was issued. This said that the President had reviewed for his conferees the latest advices from the Pacific and declared:

"It should be emphasized that the message to Congress has not yet been written and its tenor will, of course, depend on further information received between 11 o'clock tonight and noon tomorrow. Further news is coming in all the time."

Congressional leaders asserted as they left the White House that they did not know what the President would say tomorrow.

"Will the President ask for a declaration of war?" Speaker Rayburn was asked.

"He didn't say," answered the Speaker.

Asked whether Congress would support a declaration of war, Mr. Rayburn observed:

"I think that is one thing on which there would be unity."

Politics Declared Dropped

"There is no politics here," said Representative Joseph W. Martin Jr., Minority House Leader. "There is only one party when it comes to the integrity and honor of the country."

"The Republicans," said Senator Charles L. McNary of Oregon, the Senate minority leader, "will all go along, in my opinion, with whatever is done."

Unless international developments and plans changed overnight, it was indicated, the Presidential recommendations would be directed for the present, at least, at Japan only. This was asserted authoritatively in the face of widespread expectation that any

Continued on Page Six

NEWS BULLETINS
are broadcast by The New York Times every hour on the hour over Station WMCA—570 on the dial.
WEEKDAYS
8 a. m. through 11 p. m.
SUNDAYS
9 a.m., 1 p.m., 5 p.m., 11 p.m.

TOKYO ACTS FIRST

Declaration Follows Air and Sea Attacks on U. S. and Britain

TOGO CALLS ENVOYS

After Fighting Is On, Grew Gets Japan's Reply to Hull Note of Nov. 26

By The Associated Press.

TOKYO, Monday, Dec. 8—Japan went to war against the United States and Britain today with air and sea attacks against Hawaii, followed by a formal declaration of hostilities.

Japanese Imperial headquarters announced at 6 A. M. [4 P. M. Sunday, Eastern standard time] that a state of war existed among these nations in the Western Pacific, as of dawn.

Soon afterward, Domei, the Japanese official news agency, announced that "naval operations are progressing off Hawaii, with at least one Japanese aircraft carrier in action against Pearl Harbor," the American naval base in the islands.

Japanese bombers were declared to have raided Honolulu at 7:35 A. M., Hawaii time [1:05 Sunday, Eastern standard time].

Premier-War Minister General Hideki Tojo held a twenty-minute Cabinet session at his official residence at 7 A. M.

Soon afterward it was announced that both the United States Ambassador, Joseph C. Grew, and the British Ambassador, Sir Robert Leslie Craigie, had been summoned by Foreign Minister Shigenori Togo.

The Foreign Minister, Domei said, handed to Mr. Grew the Japanese Government's formal reply to the note sent to Japan by United States Secretary of State Cordell Hull on Nov. 26.

[In the course of the diplomatic negotiations leading up to yesterday's events, the Domei agency had stated that Japan could not accept the premises of Mr. Hull's note.]

Sir Robert was summoned by

Continued on Page Five

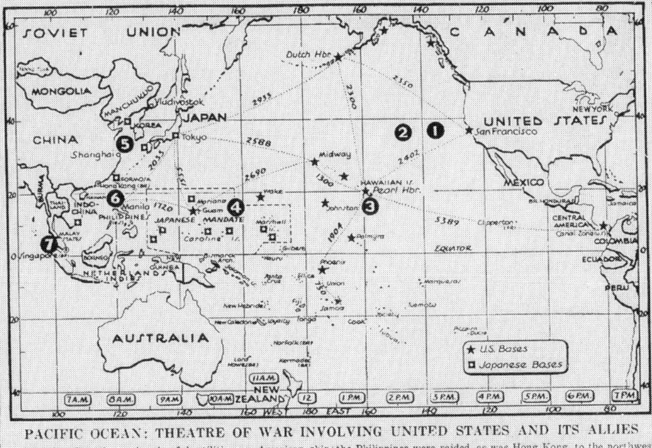

PACIFIC OCEAN: THEATRE OF WAR INVOLVING UNITED STATES AND ITS ALLIES

Shortly after the outbreak of hostilities an American ship sent a distress call from (1) and a United States Army transport carrying lumber was torpedoed at (2). The most important action was at Hawaii (3), where Japanese planes bombed the great Pearl Harbor base. Also attacked was Guam (4). From Manila (6) United States bombers roared northward, while some parts of the Philippines were raided, as was Hong Kong, to the northwest. At Shanghai (5) a British gunboat was sunk and an American gunboat seized. To the south, in the Malaya area (7), the British bombed Japanese ships, Tokyo forces attempted landings on British territory and Singapore underwent an air raid. Distances between key Pacific points are shown on the map in statute miles.

JAPANESE FORCE LANDS IN MALAYA

First Attempt Is Repulsed—Singapore Is Bombed and Thailand Invaded

By The Associated Press.

SINGAPORE, Monday, Dec. 8—The Japanese landed in Northern Malaya, 200 miles north of Singapore, today and bombed this great British naval stronghold, causing small loss of life among civilians and property damage.

About 300 Japanese troops landed on the east coast of Malaya and began filtering through jungle-fringed swamps and rice fields toward Kota Bahru airdrome, which is ten miles from the northern terminus of a railroad leading to Singapore.

An official report from the

Continued on Page Two

Tokyo Bombers Strike Hard At Our Main Bases on Oahu

By The United Press.

HONOLULU, Dec. 7—War broke with lightning suddenness in the Pacific today when waves of Japanese bombers attacked Hawaii this morning and the United States Fleet struck back with a thunder of big naval rifles. Japanese bombers, including four-engined dive bombers and torpedo-carrying planes, blasted at Pearl Harbor, the great United States naval base, the city of Honolulu and several outlying American military bases on the Island of Oahu. There were casualties of unstated number.

[The United States battleship Oklahoma was set afire by the Japanese attackers, according to a National Broadcasting Company observer, who also reported in a broadcast yesterday that two other ships in Pearl Harbor were attacked.

[The Japanese news agency, Domei, reported that the battleship Oklahoma had been sunk at Pearl Harbor, according to a United Press dispatch from Shanghai.

[Governor Joseph B. Poindexter of Hawaii talked with President Roosevelt late yesterday afternoon, saying that a second wave of Japanese bombers was just coming over, and the Gov-

Continued on Page Thirteen

ENTIRE CITY PUT ON WAR FOOTING

Japanese Rounded Up by FBI, Sent to Ellis Island—Vital Services Are Guarded

The metropolitan district reacted swiftly yesterday to the Japanese attack in the Pacific. All large communities in the area, including New York City, Newark, Jersey City, Bayonne and Paterson, went on immediate war footing.

One of the first steps taken here last night was a round-up of Japanese nationals by special agents of the Federal Bureau of Investigation, reinforced by squads of city detectives acting under FBI supervision. More than 100 FBI men, fully armed, were assigned to the detail.

The prisoners were sent to Ellis Island, where they will be held pending action at Washington. It was indicated hundreds would be detained.

Earlier Mayor La Guardia had convened his Emergency Board and directed that Japanese nationals be confined to their homes pending decision as to their status and had their clubs and other meeting places closed and put under police guard.

A police sergeant and five policemen immediately went to the Japanese Consulate at 630 Fifth Avenue in Rockefeller Center where the Consul General, Morito Morishima, and his staff were preparing to leave, and posted a guard there. The Consul General and his staff were escorted to their homes when they left. They were not to move about the city without police in attendance.

Rear Admiral Adolphus Andrews, commander of the North Atlantic Squadron, told reporters at a conference in the Federal

Continued on Page Three

FOR WANT AD RESULTS Use The New York Times. It's easy to order your ad. Just telephone LAckawanna 4-1000.—Advt.

HULL DENOUNCES TOKYO 'INFAMY'

Brands Japan 'Fraudulent' in Preparing Attack While Carrying On Parleys

Texts of Secretary Hull's note and Japan's reply, Page 10.

By BERTRAM D. HULEN
Special to THE NEW YORK TIMES.

WASHINGTON, Dec. 7—Japan was accused by Secretary of State Cordell Hull today of making a "treacherous and utterly unprovoked attack" upon the United States and of having been "infamously false and fraudulent" by preparing for the attack while conducting diplomatic negotiations with the professed desire of maintaining peace.

But even before he knew of the attack, Mr. Hull had vehemently brought the diplomatic negotiations to a virtual end with an outburst against Admiral Kichisaburo Nomura, the Japanese Ambassador, and Saburo Kurusu, special envoy, because of the insulting character of the reply they deliv-

Continued on Page Eleven

The International Situation

MONDAY, DEC. 8, 1941

Yesterday morning Japan attacked the United States at several points in the Pacific. President Roosevelt ordered United States forces into action and a declaration of war is expected this morning. [Page 1, Columns 7 and 8.] Tokyo made its declaration as of this morning against both the United States and Britain. [Page 1, Column 2.] The first Japanese assault was directed at Pearl Harbor Naval base in Hawaii. Many casualties and severe damage resulted. [Page 1, Columns 4 and 5; Map, Page 15.] United States Army aircraft took off from the Philippines this morning and some points in the Archipelago were bombed. [Page 8, Column 2.] Singapore and Hong Kong were bombed and a Japanese landing in Northern Malaya and a move on Thailand were reported. [Page 1, Column 3.] In Shanghai, Japanese marines occupied the waterfront; a British gunboat was sunk, a United States gunboat seized. [Page 9, Column 1.]

Factional lines dissolved as an angered Congress prepared to meet this morning. [Page 1, Column 1.] Secretary of State Hull accused Japan of having made a "treacherous and utterly unprovoked attack" after having been "infamously false and fraudulent." [Page 1, Column 6.] He released the text of diplomatic

while the President gave out the text of his fruitless appeal to the Japanese Emperor. [Page 12.] The White House was the hub of Washington activity and news bulletins were released there. [Page 12, Column 3.]

The Federal Bureau of Investigation was ordered to begin a round-up of some Japanese in this country. [Page 6, Column 8.] As New York City went on a war footing and public precautions were taken, the FBI began the detention of Japanese nationals. [Page 1, Column 4.]

The unification of the country under the impact of the attack was swift. [Page 6, Column 6.] Formerly conspicuous isolationists indicated full support for the war effort. [Page 6, Column 4.]

Prime Minister Churchill notified Tokyo that a state of war existed. [Page 4, Column 1.] Declarations were made last night or early today by Australia, Canada [Page 14 Column 1], the Netherlands Indies [Page 7, Column 2] and Costa Rica. [Page 15, Column 1.]

Libya was the scene of a renewed tank battle and the Tobruk corridor was reported again clear of Axis forces. [Page 20, Column 2, with map.] On the Moscow front the German line was broken at two places, said Soviet sources. [Page 17, Column 2.]

Lewis Wins Captive Mine Fight; Arbitrators Grant Union Shop

The three-man arbitration board appointed by President Roosevelt to arbitrate the union shop dispute in the captive coal mines last night reversed the decision of the National Defense Mediation Board and ruled that all workers in the captive mines should be required to join John L. Lewis's United Mine Workers as a condition of employment.

The decision was made by a two to one vote, with Benjamin F. Fairless, president of the United States Steel Corporation, dissenting. Dr. John R. Steelman, who took a leave of absence from his post as director of the United States Conciliation Service to serve as chairman of the arbitration panel, and Mr. Lewis voted in favor of extension to the captive mines of the union shop provision of the standard Appalachian agreement.

Despite his dissent, Mr. Fairless promised that the coal mining subsidiaries of United States Steel would put the ruling into effect. All eight steel companies operating captive mines had given formal assurances before the decision was reached that they would accept it as binding.

The arbitration award ended a dispute in which Mr. Lewis had repeatedly defied the President by calling strikes that menaced the production of steel and that had had its repercussions in the enactment by the House of the Smith anti-strike bill.

In explaining his vote for the union shop, Dr. Steelman pointed out that 95 per cent of the 53,000 captive miners had voluntarily assumed membership in Mr. Lewis's C. I. O. union and that 99.5 per cent of all the miners in the nation were now members of the union.

Since the bulk of the industry, including many owners of captive mines, was already operating under the union shop, it could not be argued that the United Mine Workers was endeavoring to take

Continued on Page Forty-three

SAVINGS insured up to $5,000 at Railroad Federal Savings & Loan Association, 441 Lexington Ave. (at 44th St.), N. Y. C.—Advt.

GUAM BOMBED; ARMY SHIP IS SUNK

U. S. Fliers Head North From Manila—Battleship Oklahoma Set Afire by Torpedo Planes at Honolulu

104 SOLDIERS KILLED AT FIELD IN HAWAII

President Fears 'Very Heavy Losses' on Oahu—Churchill Notifies Japan That a State of War Exists

By FRANK L. KLUCKHOHN
Special to THE NEW YORK TIMES.

WASHINGTON, Monday, Dec. 8—Sudden and unexpected attacks on Pearl Harbor, Honolulu, and other United States possessions in the Pacific early yesterday by the Japanese air force and navy plunged the United States and Japan into active war.

The initial attack in Hawaii, apparently launched by torpedo-carrying bombers and submarines, caused widespread damage and death. It was quickly followed by others. There were unconfirmed reports that German raiders participated in the attacks.

Guam also was assaulted from the air, as were Davao, on the island of Mindanao, and Camp John Hay, in Northern Luzon, both in the Philippines. Lieut. Gen. Douglas MacArthur, commanding the United States Army of the Far East, reported there was little damage, however.

[Japanese parachute troops had been landed in the Philippines and native Japanese had seized some communities, Royal Arch Gunnison said in a broadcast from Manila today to WOR-Mutual. He reported without detail that "in the naval war the ABCD fleets under American command appeared to be successful" against Japanese invasions.]

Japanese submarines, ranging out over the Pacific, sank an American transport carrying lumber 1,300 miles from San Francisco, and distress signals were heard from a freighter 700 miles from that city.

The War Department reported that 104 soldiers died and 300 were wounded as a result of the attack on Hickam Field, Hawaii. The National Broadcasting Company reported from Honolulu that the battleship Oklahoma was afire. [Domei, Japanese news agency, reported the Oklahoma sunk.]

Nation Placed on Full War Basis

The news of these surprise attacks fell like a bombshell on Washington. President Roosevelt immediately ordered the country and the Army and Navy onto a full war footing. He arranged at a White House conference last night to address a joint session of Congress at noon today, presumably to ask for declaration of a formal state of war.

This was disclosed after a long special Cabinet meeting, which was joined later by Congressional leaders. These leaders predicted "action" within a day.

After leaving the White House conference Attorney General Francis Biddle said that "a resolution" would be introduced in Congress tomorrow. He would not amplify or affirm that it would be for a declaration of war.

Congress probably will "act" within the day, and he will call the Senate Foreign Relations Committee for this purpose, Chairman Tom Connally announced.

[A United Press dispatch from London this morning said that Prime Minister Churchill had notified Japan that a state of war existed.]

As the reports of heavy fighting flashed into the White House, London reported semi-officially that the British Empire would carry out Prime Minister Winston Churchill's pledge to give the United States full support in case of hostilities with Japan. The President and Mr. Churchill talked by transatlantic telephone.

This was followed by a statement in London from the Netherland Government in Exile that it considered a state of war to exist between the Netherlands and Japan. Canada, Australia and Costa Rica took similar action.

Landing Made in Malaya

A Singapore communiqué disclosed that Japanese troops had landed in Northern Malaya and that Singapore had been bombed.

The President told those at last night's White House meeting that "doubtless very heavy losses" were sustained by the Navy and also by the Army on the island of Oahu [Honolulu]. It was impossible to obtain confirmation or denial of reports that the battleships Oklahoma and West Virginia had been damaged or sunk at Pearl Harbor, together with six or seven destroyers, and that 350 United States airplanes had been caught on the ground.

The White House took over control of the bulletins, and the Navy Department, therefore, said it could not discuss the matter or answer any questions how the Japanese were able to penetrate the Hawaiian defenses or appear without previous knowledge of their presence in those waters.

Administration circles forecast that the United States soon might be involved in a world-wide war, with Germany supporting Japan, an Axis partner. The German official radio tonight attacked the United States and supported Japan.

Axis diplomats here expressed complete surprise that the Japanese had attacked. But the impression gained from their attitude was that they believed it represented a victory for the Nazi attempt to divert lease-lend aid from Britain, which has been

Continued on Page Four

Fire and wreckage at the Naval Air Station in Pearl Harbor.

Three civilians were killed in this shrapnel-riddled car during the attack.

from the north. Then men on other ships spotted them. At first, some thought they were army or navy planes taking part in drills. But these planes had red circles painted on the wings and fuselages. These planes were Japanese.

As the crewmen on the ships stared upward in disbelief, the planes swung into action. Torpedo planes glided toward the big ships. Dive-bombers plunged down to attack the planes lined up at Wheeler Field, Hickam Field, and the other bases. After each plane delivered its bombs, it circled back to spray its target with machine-gun fire.

As the bombs exploded, concrete, glass, dirt, and sheets of metal flew in every direction. Smoke erupted from ships, airfields, and docks. Guns barked.

On board the battleship *Oklahoma*, the air-raid alert sounded and someone's voice blared over the ship's PA system: "Real planes, real bombs; this is no drill!" Hardly had the crew been warned, when a torpedo struck. A second torpedo blast put out the lights. Three more ripped open the ship's hull, sending the vessel to the bottom of the harbor.

Right after the *Oklahoma* went down, the battleship *Arizona* was hit. A bomb exploded in the forward magazine, where ammunition was stored. A witness said the ship looked "like an earthquake had struck it." Of the 1,400 men aboard the *Arizona*, fewer than 200 survived.

The assault started a few minutes before eight o'clock and lasted until 8:25. Then a second wave of attackers, made up of dive-bombers and high-level bombers, struck.

Aircraft destroyed as a result of the bombing.

Thousands of Americans learned of the Pearl Harbor attack while listening to the broadcast of a pro football game in New York.

In all, the attacks lasted two hours. But it was the torpedo bombers in the first wave that did the most damage.

The *Arizona* sank, *Oklahoma* capsized, and *West Virginia,* hit by torpedoes, settled in the mud. *California* went to the bottom, too.

Two other battleships were badly damaged. Three destroyers and four smaller vessels were also sunk. Of the American aircraft, 188 were destroyed and 63 damaged.

On some ships and shore stations, anti-aircraft guns answered the attack. But there were too few of them and they were too late getting into action. The Japanese lost only 29 of the 350 planes that took part in the raid. The six aircraft carriers that had launched the planes were never touched.

American casualties were 2,400 killed and more than 1,000 wounded. Japanese killed and wounded came to less than 100.

While the bombing succeeded in putting the U.S. Pacific Fleet out of action and giving the Japanese control of the central Pacific, the attack missed the fleet's aircraft carriers, which happened to be at sea. The carriers would play an important role in the months ahead.

Nearly every American who was alive that day can describe how he or she first heard the news of the attack. In that regard, the day Pearl Harbor was bombed is like the day in November 1963 when President John F. Kennedy was shot. The moment is engraved in virtually everyone's memory.

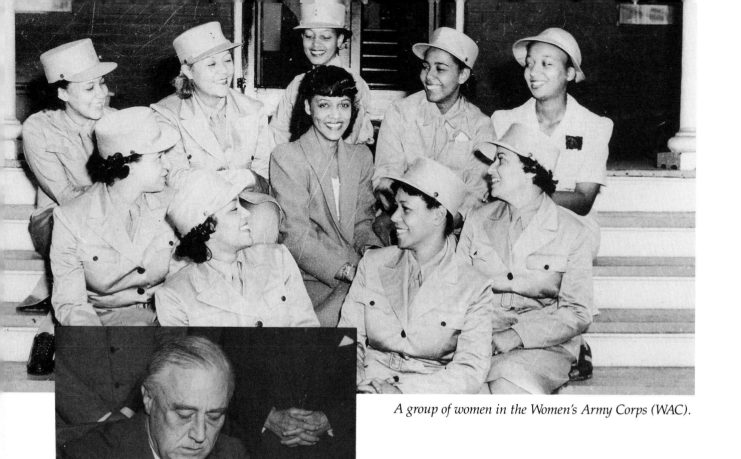

A group of women in the Women's Army Corps (WAC).

On December 8, 1941, President Roosevelt signs the declaration of war against Japan.

America Goes to War

On the day after Pearl Harbor was bombed, Franklin Delano Roosevelt, the 32nd President of the United States, addressed Congress. He stood alone at the rostrum, reading pages from a black looseleaf notebook. He began:

"Yesterday, December 7, 1941 — a date which will live in infamy — the United States of America was suddenly and deliberately attacked . . ."

The President's speech lasted six minutes. Within the next hour, Congress voted to declare war on Japan. There was only one "no" vote.

Three days later, Germany and Italy, Japan's allies in Europe, declared war on the United States, and then Congress de-

Women served in many branches of the United States Armed Forces.

Troops being given a warm farewell as they head off into battle.

clared war on Germany and Italy. Together, Germany, Italy, and Japan were known as the Axis powers.

In the days following the Pearl Harbor attack, volunteers flooded recruiting stations to sign up. The United States also used draft laws to build its military strength. Some 16 million men and women would serve in the Army, Navy, Marine Corps, and Coast Guard.

Women in the Army belonged to a special unit called the Women's Army Corps (WAC). The women who served were known as Wacs. At its peak, the WAC included some 100,000 enlisted women and officers. Navy women were known as Waves, an abbreviation for Women Accepted for Volunteer Emergency Service.

The nation turned its industrial might toward winning the war. Millions of Americans went to work in war industries. Guns, planes, tanks, and ships were turned out in tremendous quantities.

The United States was compared to a "sleeping giant." The giant had been awakened by Pearl Harbor and was angry. That anger was focused on the Japanese. For Japan and its allies, that meant their ultimate defeat.

In the summer of 1939, a Chinese woman sobs after Japanese planes destroyed her home in a bombing raid north of Chunking.

Adolf Hitler, mapping strategy with his generals.

Aggression on the March

For the United States, World War II began with the attack on Pearl Harbor on December 7, 1941. But for many other nations of the world, it had begun years earlier.

Some historians consider the starting date of World War II to be September 18, 1931. That's when Japan, a nation then dominated by military leaders and later to be headed by General Hideki Tojo, seized Manchuria (now the northeastern provinces of China). Once in control of Manchuria, the Japanese set up a puppet state called Manchukuo.

Hitler was well prepared for war, with vast armored and motorized divisions.

The Japanese invaded China near Shanghai in 1932, withdrew, and then launched a full-scale invasion in 1937, overrunning large areas of northern China. By the end of 1938, the Japanese controlled most of China's ports and industrial cities.

As the fighting in China died down, the Japanese eyed other goals — rubber, tin, rice, oil, and other riches of southeast Asia. In September 1940, Japanese troops marched into Indochina (now Vietnam, Laos, and Kampuchea). Burma and Malaya, then under British rule, the Dutch East Indies, and even the Philippine Is-

lands were set as future targets by the Japanese. As they expanded their influence, tensions between Japan and the United States kept mounting.

In Italy, Benito Mussolini ruled as dictator. His ambition was to build a great Italian colonial empire. In 1935, Mussolini's troops invaded Ethiopia, using tanks and bombers against Ethiopian tribesmen and their antiquated rifles. By 1936, Mussolini could proclaim himself "Emperor of Ethiopia." In 1939, Mussolini ordered the invasion of Albania.

Throughout much of Europe during this

Hitler, grinning, meets with members of the Nazi youth group.

German troops roll into Prague, Czechoslovakia, in 1939.

period, the focus was on Adolf Hitler, who ruled Germany as dictator. Hitler had come to power in 1933 as head of the National Socialist, or Nazi, Party. A spell-binding speaker with the ability to arouse huge groups of people, Hitler promised the German people, still smarting from losses suffered in World War I, that he would win back their lands and restore the nation to its past glory.

Hitler told the Germans that the nation's defeat in World War I was chiefly the fault of the Jews. After Hitler came to power, the German government passed laws depriving Jews of their rights and possessions. Jews were forced to live in special areas called ghettos and made to work as slave laborers. Later the Nazis launched a campaign of mass murder against all the Jews of Europe.

Hitler's first aggressive move took place in March 1938 when he ordered German forces into Austria. There was no resistance; it was over quickly. Hitler made

Italian dictator Benito Mussolini.

Nazi officers oversee the transport by cattle car of Jewish people to concentration camps.

Austria a part of Germany.

Hitler's next target was Czechoslovakia in a region called the Sudetenland. Hitler demanded the Sudetenland be placed under German rule. The Czechs refused and got ready to fight. Russia promised to support Czechoslovakia if Germany attacked.

With Europe on the brink of a war, Great Britain's Prime Minister Neville Chamberlain and French Premier Édouard Daladier went to Munich in Germany to meet with Hitler and Mussolini. The four signed an agreement giving Hitler what he wanted.

Under the terms of the treaty, Czechoslovakia lost the Sudetenland to Germany. The Czechs, none of whom had been permitted to attend the conference, had been betrayed.

Chamberlain returned to London, proclaiming the Munich Pact meant "peace in our time." Chamberlain could not have been more wrong.

German troops enter the Danish city of Aalborg.

Blitzkrieg!

London newspapers scream news of Hitler's attack.

In March 1939, Germany took over the rest of Czechoslovakia. Once Czechoslovakia was in his control, Hitler called his generals together and told them Poland was next on the list.

The French and British promised to stand by Poland in the event of a German attack. That didn't matter to Hitler. On September 1, 1939, Germany's armies attacked Poland, pioneering a new kind of warfare called *blitzkrieg*, or "lightning war." Fast-moving tanks and armored vehicles smashed their way through the Polish fighting forces. Stuka dive-bombers came screaming out of the sky to attack Polish troops and blast road junctions and rail lines. Heavier planes rained bombs on Warsaw, the Polish capital.

In a matter of weeks, Poland was on the brink of collapse. Russia had signed a nonaggression pact with Germany in August 1939. On September 17, the Soviet Union, now Germany's ally, attacked Poland from the east. Ten days later, all Polish resistance ended.

The French and British had entered the war as they had promised. But before they could put any pressure on the German forces, it was too late.

Hitler confers with his generals during the battle of Warsaw, the Polish capital.

Captured British soldiers are marched through the city of Trondheim, Norway, by the victorious Germans.

In the months that followed the fall of Poland, the French dug in behind the Maginot Line, a long series of heavily fortified bunkers along the border between France and Germany. The Germans sat behind their opposing Siegfried Line. There they awaited Hitler's orders to attack.

The six months of calm that followed the German conquest of Poland ended suddenly early in April 1940 when Hitler's forces struck again. Norway was the target. German troops, ferried on warships, landed at the Norwegian capital of Oslo and at several other cities along the coast.

While this was taking place, German forces also invaded Denmark, where they faced little resistance. Denmark surrendered almost immediately.

The Norwegians fought but they were caught by surprise. And once the Germans were ashore, they brought in wave after wave of reinforcements and heavy weapons. The Norwegians were overwhelmed

before they could organize.

Great Britain and France sent troops to Norway but since the German planes controlled the skies, the troops were of little value and were soon evacuated. On June 9, 1940, the Norwegian Army surrendered to the Germans.

It was another stunning victory for Hitler, whose forces had moved swiftly and boldly. By comparison, the Allies were confused and inept. With their victory, the Germans now had air and naval bases from which they would later be able to attack Allied shipping heading north to the Soviet Union.

But the German victory had a price. British warships had inflicted heavy losses on the German navy during the campaign.

One other result of the Allied defeat in Norway was a change in command. Winston Churchill replaced Neville Chamberlain as Prime Minister of England. Energetic and fearless, the round-faced Churchill gave the British the leadership they sought.

17

Adolf Hitler gives the Nazi salute to cheering crowds.

Retreat to Dunkirk

E ven before Norway had surrendered, the German war machine was on the move in western Europe. In the early dawn of May 10, 1940, German armored units knifed into Belgium, Luxembourg, and the Netherlands. At the same time, Hitler's airplanes attacked airfields and communications centers. In five days, the Germans overran the Netherlands. Luxembourg fell in one day. Before the end of May, Belgium surrendered.

Now the northeastern corner of France, guarded by French and British troops, was in danger. Hitler sent an armored column racing westward toward the English Channel, the idea being to cut off the French and British forces, trapping them.

Thousands of French troops arrive in England after crossing the English Channel from Dunkirk.

British troops being evacuated at Dunkirk, on the northern French coast.

The French and British retreated to Dunkirk, the only port on the northern French coast not in German hands. German forces pressed the French and British from every side. There was no alternative but to evacuate.

Across the English Channel, the British government organized everything that would float. Destroyers, minesweepers, tugboats, ferryboats, fishing boats, yachts, dories, dinghies, and motor launches set out for Dunkirk, 32 miles away. While the Royal Air Force provided protection, British, French, Belgian, and Dutch troops waded out to the rescue fleet. Each time a boat sailed back to England, it would return for another load. More than 330,000 troops escaped.

While the Allies had suffered a military disaster, they were not beaten. Winston Churchill gave proof of that. After Dunkirk, he declared: "We shall fight on the seas and oceans. We shall fight with growing confidence and growing strength in the air. We shall defend our island, whatever the cost may be. We shall fight on the beaches. We shall fight on the landing grounds. We shall fight in the fields and the streets. We shall fight in the hills. We shall never surrender!"

German soldiers under fire in France during the spring of 1940.

The Fall of France

With the British forces driven back to their island home, the French Army, facing the Germans alone, quickly collapsed in confusion. With the French defeat obvious, Mussolini decided it was time for Italy to join in and ordered an attack on the southern French seacoast.

On June 14, 1940, less than two weeks after the British evacuation at Dunkirk, German troops marched into Paris. On June 22, France surrendered.

Hitler was less than gracious in victory. He ordered that the armistice talks be held in the same railway car in Compiègne Forest where the Germans had signed surrender terms in 1918 following World War I. After the French delegation had signed the armistice, Hitler is said to have danced a victory jig outside the railway car. He then ordered it to be hauled off to Germany.

Between September 1939 and June 1940, Hitler's armies overran seven European nations — Poland, Norway, Denmark, Holland, Belgium, Luxembourg, and France.

The German army parades in Paris, June, 1940, following the fall of France.

With the surrender of France, Hitler ruled throughout northern Europe. In six weeks, he had conquered the Norwegians, Danes, Belgians, Dutch, Luxembourgers, and French. Nazi rulers were put into power in all the occupied countries. Only the southern part of France was allowed a limited form of self-government.

The British now stood alone in Europe. Hitler hoped that the British would realize their hopeless military situation and accept surrender terms. But Winston Churchill rejected any idea of negotiating with Hitler. Still, Hitler felt Churchill was bluffing and continued to wait.

But Churchill was not bluffing. When, in July 1940, Hitler began to realize this, he ordered his generals to prepare to invade England. The invasion was called "Operation Sea Lion."

Fires rage out of control in blacked-out London following a German bomber attack.

The Battle of Britain

Before Hitler's troops could cross the English Channel from France and land on British soil, it was vital for the Germans to have command of the air. So began a desperate battle in the skies over Great Britain.

Night after night, wave after wave of Stuka dive-bombers, Dorniers, and Heinkels roared over the English Channel to drop their deadly cargoes. At first, the

A German bomber downed during the Battle of Britain.

Prime Minister Winston Churchill is greeted by British workers after inspecting the bomb damage in the city of Birmingham.

German planes attacked ports and docking facilities. Then they switched to airfields. For a time, the city of London served as the prime target. On the afternoon of September 7, 1940, nearly a thousand German aircraft rained their bombs on London.

The British stood up to the bombardment. They did not panic. They slept in subways. They fought the fires. English children were evacuated to the countryside or sent to Canada or elsewhere.

The British defended their island gallantly. A radar net gave them an early warning when German planes were on their way. It was primitive by standards of today — but it worked.

*At Westminster Abbey, massive piles of sandbags protect
the famous tombs of kings and queens against damage by
air raids.*

A group of British children — refugees from the war zone — arrive in New York. They are the first of many children to be evacuated from England under an American plan to provide them with safe homes until the war ends.

This photograph reveals the devastation wreaked by Nazi bombers in London.

The British sent their fast Spitfire and Hurricane fighter planes into the air to intercept the German bombers. Each was equipped with eight American Browning machine guns mounted in the wings. The young and courageous Royal Air Force pilots downed more than a thousand German planes.

By the fall of 1940, it was obvious that the Germans were not going to win the Battle of Britain. German planes could not destroy the Royal Air Force's strength or the people's morale. Hitler called off the invasion of England.

A fighter squadron operations room during the Battle of Britain.

German troops move through snow and wind in the Ukraine.

Hitler Invades Russia

E arly in June 1940, while Hitler's forces were attempting to pin down their victory in France, Soviet leader Joseph Stalin seized the opportunity to occupy the Baltic states of Lithuania, Estonia, and Latvia. Earlier, in late 1939, the Soviet Union had invaded Finland. The Finns surrendered to the Russians in March 1940.

Stalin's occupation of the Baltic states and other aggressive acts made Hitler uneasy. He began planning an attack on the Soviet Union, even though Germany and the Soviet Union were treaty partners.

Soviet leader Joseph Stalin (right) confers with Voycheslao Molotov, foreign minister.

Near Beschnkowitsch in the Soviet Union, German troops create a cloud of smoke to cover their movements.

On June 22, 1941, Hitler ordered a three-million-man army to launch an all-out assault on the Soviet Union. The battle line stretched all the way from the Arctic to the Black Sea, a distance of some two thousand miles.

The invasion took the Russians by surprise. At first, Hitler's armies made spectacular headway with their *blitzkrieg* tactics. Their motorized columns broke through the battle lines time after time, creating pockets of Soviet troops who were then forced to surrender. Within less than a month, the Germans had driven 450 miles into Russia.

But the tide of battle began to change during the Russian winter of 1941–42. One reason was Hitler's mistake in estimating Soviet manpower. The Russians mobilized troops by the millions. Beginning late in 1941, German troops on the Russian front were almost always outnumbered.

Mud, snow, and the bitter cold also worked to stall the German advance. German troops got as far as the outskirts of Moscow, but there Russian defenders turned them back.

Hitler had been so confident, he believed he would conquer Russia in six weeks. German soldiers had not even been issued winter uniforms. But when Russian resistance stiffened late in 1941, Hitler knew he could no longer hope for an easy victory.

As part of America's lend-lease program, an American locomotive is unloaded in Iran before shipment to the Soviet Union.

The United States: Arsenal of Democracy

After war broke out in Europe in 1939, Americans debated what role their nation should play in the conflict. While the great majority of Americans supported Great Britain, France, and the other European democratic nations, few people thought the United States should go to war on their behalf.

Franklin D. Roosevelt, who took his third presidential oath of office in January 1941, called upon the United States to be "the great arsenal of democracy." He wanted America to supply what aid it could to the Allied nations. In March 1941, Congress passed the Lend Lease Act. It gave Roosevelt the power to provide goods and services to Great Britain, the Soviet Union, and other Allied countries that he thought to be vital to the defense of the United States.

American "isolationists" opposed this policy. They believed the United States should avoid war at any cost. They felt that supplying war materials to European nations could not help but draw the United States into the conflict.

In August 1941, President Roosevelt and Prime Minister Churchill held a historic meeting on board a warship off Newfoundland. There they signed the Atlantic Charter, a statement of their war aims, in which the two men pledged to respect the right of every nation to choose its own form of government. The Atlantic Charter became one of the building blocks of the charter of the United Nations.

Although the United States was still not at war, the U.S. Navy had become involved in the fighting. Navy vessels had been assigned to escort merchant ships carrying war goods across the Atlantic

President Roosevelt (left) greets British Prime Minister Churchill at Placentia Bay, Newfoundland, for the beginning of the Atlantic Conference. At center is Roosevelt's son, Elliot.

Isolationists rallied in an effort to keep America out of the war.

Ocean as far as Iceland, where the Royal Navy took over. As a result, Navy destroyers began to clash with German submarines.

In September 1941, a German submarine fired a torpedo at the *Greer*, a U.S. destroyer. It missed; the *Greer* then attacked the submarine with depth charges. They missed, too. But the incident marked the first time the United States and Germany exchanged shots.

Late in October 1941, a German submarine torpedoed the *Reuben James*, another American destroyer, sending it to the bottom. Nearly 100 lives were lost. The *Reuben James* was the first American naval vessel lost as a result of enemy action in World War II.

The debate concerning the nation's role in the war got hotter. Yet most Americans still believed the war was not their war. Some isolationists called Roosevelt a warmonger.

On December 7, 1941, the debate ended. The bombing of Pearl Harbor united the nation as no event before or since. The country's 130 million people dedicated themselves to the defeat of Japan, Germany, and Italy. And they had a rallying cry. It was: "Remember Pearl Harbor!"

A U.S. plane over Wake Island in the Pacific. It fell to the Japanese early in the war.

Japan's Pacific Conquests

Pearl Harbor was not Japan's only target on December 7, 1941. The next day, Japanese bombers struck American bases in the central Pacific, including Wake Island and Guam. After the bombings, Japanese troops moved in.

The Japanese also bombed Midway Island and Manila, the capital of the Philippine Islands. On December 10, tens of thousands of Japanese troops invaded the Philippines, landing on Luzon, the main island. The poorly equipped Philippine Army was no match for the Japanese.

General Douglas MacArthur, commander of U.S. Army forces in the Far East, withdrew his troops to the Bataan Peninsula that juts into Manila Bay on the southwestern coast of Luzon. The

Jubilant Japanese troops brandish samurai swords and flags after their victory in the Philippines.

Weary Allied defenders of Corregidor, an island fortress in Manila Bay in the Philippines, are marched to prison camps by victorious Japanese.

Japanese general Masa Haru Homma on an inspection tour of his Philippine command in 1944.

Philippine and American forces were pushed down the peninsula until they were forced to surrender. MacArthur left the Philippines by torpedo boat, promising, "I shall return." By May 6, 1942, all resistance in the Philippines had ended.

The Japanese forced about sixty thousand Philippine and American prisoners to march seventy miles to prison camps. It was inhuman. The prisoners of war were brutally mistreated by the Japanese. Called the Bataan Death March, it resulted in the death of ten thousand sick and starving prisoners.

In addition to their conquest of Wake Island, Guam, and the Philippines, the Japanese swept down the Malay Peninsula and captured Singapore. They occupied Burma and took Hong Kong. They overran the Dutch East Indies.

For years, the Japanese had dreamed of building a vast empire in the central Pacific and southeast Asia. Now that dream was becoming a reality.

The surprise bombing attack on Japan was launched from the flight deck of the carrier <u>Hornet</u>.

America Strikes Back

Once the Philippines had fallen, the Japanese empire stretched halfway across the Pacific from Japan, threatening Hawaii and the island of Midway. In the southwest Pacific, Japan even menaced Australia.

But before the Japanese could make another move, their plans were interrupted by a bold American bombing raid. Early in April 1942, the aircraft carrier *Hornet* sailed from San Francisco toward Japan. About 650 miles from Tokyo, the carrier's 16 twin-engine B-25 Mitchell

As the gun crew watches, a B-25 bomber lumbers into the air. Its target: Japan, about 650 miles to the west.

bombers were ordered into the air. Each plane had a 2,000-pound bomb-load. The B-25s reached Japan in about four hours, dropping their bombs on the cities of Tokyo, Nagoya, and Kobe. Then the planes flew on to China, where the crews either had to crash-land or drop by parachute. Out of the 82 crew members, 70 survived.

The daring raid gave a big boost to American morale, which had been badly damaged by Pearl Harbor. It shocked the

American losses at Midway include the carrier <u>Yorktown</u> (above), a victim of Japanese bombs and torpedoes.

Twenty-six-year-old John F. Kennedy, a Navy lieutenant, was twice decorated by the Navy for his exploits as a PT boat captain in the Pacific in 1943. Kennedy would later become the nation's thirty-fifth president.

Japanese. They did not believe that Allied bombers would ever reach their home islands. Now they realized they were vulnerable to attack and would have to keep valuable aircraft in reserve to ward off future raids.

The attack on their homeland did little to halt the Japanese advance, however. Their next objectives were Midway Island, about 1,100 miles west of Hawaii, and the Aleutian Islands, part of Alaska.

On June 4, 1942, aircraft from Japanese

A Douglas Dauntless dive-bomber on the attack during the Battle of Midway.

carriers began blasting Midway, softening up the island for the invasion that was to follow. But unknown to the Japanese, three American carriers, the *Hornet*, *Enterprise*, and *Yorktown*, were sitting to the north of Midway. While the Japanese planes were bombing Midway, American dive-bombers and torpedo bombers hit the invasion fleet. The battle lasted two days. When it ended, the Japanese had lost 4 aircraft carriers as well as some 330 aircraft.

American losses included 1 carrier, the *Yorktown*, and about 150 aircraft.

Although the Japanese were forced to withdraw from Midway, their other invasion force succeeded in capturing two of the Aleutian Islands, Kiska and Attu. The Japanese later also occupied Agattu. These bleak and rocky islands, often covered by fog, had no strategic value. By the spring of the next year, they were back in American hands.

Smoke billows from the <u>Yorktown</u> as crew members struggle to save the ship.

While the struggle for the islands in the Aleutian chain has all but been forgotten, the Battle of Midway has not. For the first time, the Americans had won a clearcut victory in head-to-head combat with the Imperial Navy. No longer would the Japanese be looked upon as a superior force in the Pacific; the balance had been restored. Midway was the turning point that spelled Japan's eventual defeat.

Two Native-American marines stationed in Guam.

Guadalcanal

American military leaders were eager to follow up the victory at Midway by launching a counteroffensive in the Pacific. They had watched while the Japanese had assembled a huge empire in the Pacific. Now it was time to go on the attack.

On August 7, 1942, U.S. Marines landed on the island of Guadalcanal, one of the southernmost of the Solomon Islands in the southwest Pacific, not far from Australia. At first, there was little resistance from the Japanese. The Marines quickly captured the island's airfield, one of the operation's chief goals.

But the Japanese began occupying the island from nearby bases, and soon the fighting turned brutal. Japanese riflemen

A U.S. Army unit at Guadalcanal advances toward the front.

Unloading a Marine Corps tank at Guadalcanal.

and machine gunners were not the only problems. American troops had to learn to cope with the wet, smelly, silent jungle and the torrential rains that turned the black soil into thick mud and made the roads unusable.

Japanese soldiers were fanatical. Following the ancient code of *bushido*, they fought to the death. To surrender was to be disgraced. Japanese soldiers often committed suicide rather than allow themselves to be captured.

There were countless American heroes. Private Joe Wadsworth was one. He fired at a wave of attacking Japanese with an automatic rifle, hitting several, until his gun jammed. He picked up a rifle and fired with that. When the Japanese got close, he jumped up and met them with his bayonet. He was struck with a bullet that knocked him down. He refused to be moved to an aid station until the more seriously injured could be cared for.

Guadalcanal was a long struggle. Not until February 1943 were the Japanese troops driven from the island. The U.S. built up its strength on Guadalcanal and used the island as a stepping-stone for the invasion of other Japanese strongholds in the southwest Pacific.

The SS <u>Benson</u> after being torpedoed by a German submarine.

The U-boat Threat

From the earliest days of the war, German submarines, called U-boats (for undersea boats), were a deadly menace to Allied ships crossing the Atlantic Ocean. During the first six months of 1942, U-boats sank no fewer than 500 Allied merchant ships. The sinkings continued throughout the war. Not until the very end did they stop.

As a means of self-protection, Allied vessels traveled in convoys, with each convoy consisting of as many as 40 or 50 freighters and tankers. The convoy vessels were guarded by a handful of destroyers, destroyer escorts, and other ships armed with depth charges and light guns.

Allied convoys were made up of scores of ships, which were guarded by destroyers, destroyer escorts, and other armed vessels.

At first, each U-boat operated on its own, but later group tactics were used. Several U-boats would band together in a "wolf pack," and when a convoy was spotted, the subs would wait until nightfall and then attack the vessels one by one.

Eventually the Allies gained the upper hand in the Battle of the Atlantic. Improved radar and sonar enabled escort vessels to detect submarines with great efficiency. The escort carrier, which featured a flight deck built on a merchant ship hull, was another important factor. When a U-boat was detected, escort carrier aircraft could be launched to attack it.

The Allies began sinking U-boats at a much faster rate than the Germans could build them. By 1944, the U-boat threat had diminished, but Allied ships still had to keep up their guard.

The closer the Germans got to Stalingrad (now Volgograd) the harder the Russians fought.

Russia's vastness and Arctic temperatures helped to slow the German advance.

The Battle of Stalingrad

In the spring of 1942, Hitler revealed a simple battle plan that he hoped would lead to victory in the Soviet Union. He would open a fresh campaign in the south, his goals being to capture the city of Stalingrad on the Volga River and the oilfields of Caucasus. Hitler reasoned that once the Germans controlled Russia's petroleum supplies, the Soviet war machine would grind to a halt.

The closer the Germans got to Stalingrad (now Volgograd), the tougher the Russians fought. Although the German troops managed to force their way into the city, the Russians would not give up. Through the fall and into the winter, German and Soviet soldiers fought hand to hand from behind piles of brick and mortar. They battled for every room, every cellar, every street.

Lieutenant General von Daniel (center) of the German Army, one of the many Nazi commanders captured by the Russians at Stalingrad, passes a dead German as he surrenders with what is left of his troops.

Herded together by their Russian captors, Nazi soldiers march around the outskirts of bombed-out Stalingrad. When the Russians broke the siege of this city, they captured the remnants of 22 German divisions, including 24 generals.

When the Volga River froze, Soviet troops brought up reinforcements and supplies at night. Russians who crossed the river were told not to come back.

The battle raged for five months. Hitler pleaded with his generals not to give up. The Russians were just as determined to hold on.

Late in November, Soviet armies surrounded the German units in and near the city. Hitler sent more troops to free the encircled Germans, but the relief units could not penetrate the Soviet lines.

The Germans hung on grimly during the brutal winter. Early in February, resistance ended. Only 90,000 hungry, half-frozen troops remained out of an original force of more than a quarter of a million.

The great struggle for Stalingrad was a dramatic turning point in World War II. It signaled the beginning of the end for German forces in Russia.

The North African invasion forces were commanded by an American, General Dwight D. Eisenhower. He would later become the thirty-fourth president of the United States.

"Operation Torch"

In the spring of 1941, with Hitler in control of almost all of continental Europe, North Africa took on enormous strategic importance. Along with Great Britain and the Soviet Union, North Africa provided a jumping-off point from which attacks on Hitler's "Fortress Europe" could be launched.

The British had troops stationed in Egypt before the war began. While British forces had won important victories in North Africa, Axis armies still posed a threat to Egypt, the Suez Canal, and the oil riches of the Middle East.

The British realized that to win in North Africa the Allies would have to mount an invasion. The Americans reluctantly

Major General George S. Patton (with two stars on his helmet) goes ashore during the Allied campaign in North Africa.

The aircraft carrier <u>Chenango</u> delivers P-40 pursuit planes for the North African invasion.

agreed. The invasion was given the code name "Operation Torch."

On November 8, 1942, troops, tanks, and tons of supplies were put ashore safely from a vast fleet of ships which had sailed from the United States and Great Britain. American forces landed near Casablanca in Morocco and Oran in Algeria. British troops, along with Americans, went ashore at Algiers in Algeria.

Little by little, the Allies pressed the German and Italian troops back, although there was some bitter fighting. American forces advanced eastward across Algeria toward Tunisia, while the British pushed into southern Tunisia. In an effort to stave off defeat, Hitler poured reinforcements into Tunisia from Sicily and Italy, just across the Mediterranean Sea. But the Allies kept advancing, forcing the Germans and Italians back against the sea. When the enemy forces surrendered on May 12, 1943, 200,000 prisoners fell into Allied hands.

Loaded with Navy men, this Coast Guard landing barge heads for the Sicilian shore.

The Invasion of Italy

The Allies moved fast to take advantage of the Axis collapse in North Africa. On July 10, 1943, powerful American and British armies crossed from North African bases to land on the island of Sicily, just west of Italy's southern tip. They quickly overran enemy beach defenses. By mid-August, Sicily was in Allied hands. "It is the beginning of the end," President Roosevelt declared.

American troops on board one of the many Landing Ship-Tanks (LSTs), heading for Sicily.

The next move was obvious. Italy lay right across the Straits of Messina. On September 3, 1943, British troops crossed the narrow band of water and landed in southern Italy. A few days later, American forces stormed ashore at Salerno, south of Naples on Italy's west coast. The plan was for the two armies to link up and then push their way up the Italian "boot."

But the invasion did not go as planned. Allied forces were slowed by the mountainous terrain and bad weather. In four months, the Allies advanced only seventy miles beyond Salerno. One Allied commander described the campaign as "slogging up Italy."

The campaign produced one great benefit, however. Italian people had grown

German soldiers captured in Sicily are marched off to prison camp.

tired of the war. They felt the fighting had become pointless. During the fighting in Sicily, Italian dictator Benito Mussolini fell from power and was imprisoned. Italy's prime minister then entered into peace negotiations with the Allies. Shortly after, Italy surrendered.

Despite this, Hitler had no thought of giving up Italy to the Allies. He rushed

Members of a mortar company shell German troops near Massa, Italy.

troops and supplies into Italy to reinforce German forces.

By the opening months of 1944, the campaign had reached a stalemate. Allied hopes for a quick victory in Italy had been dashed. The Allies' goal now was to keep as many German soldiers as possible pinned down so they could not be used elsewhere.

A B-17 Flying Fortress over its target: warehouses and a railroad junction in Romania.

While Flying Fortresses bombed during daylight hours, these British Lancasters bombed at night.

The Air War to Cripple German Industries

Air power did not bring about the defeat of Hitler's Germany. But the Allied victory in Europe could not have been won without it.

British and American air forces began launching their huge four-engine bombers from bases in England in 1942. The British, with their Stirlings, Halifaxes, and Lancasters, bombed at night, sending as many as a thousand bombers at one time over a target, causing the widest possible devastation.

American bomber pilots flew B-17 Flying Fortresses and B-24 Liberators. They attacked during daylight hours, hitting selective targets — oil refineries, power plants, aircraft plants, and the like — from high altitudes.

The Allies were capable of wiping out whole cities with their bombers — and sometimes they did. Between July and November in 1943, the German seaport city of Hamburg was the target in 33 major bombing raids. In several of the attacks, more than 700 planes took part. During one raid the vast number of explosive and incendiary bombs that went off in the center of the city created a fierce firestorm — "a fire typhoon such as never before witnessed," said one observer. The

Members of the historic all-Black Tuskegee Airmen.

A grim-faced Hitler inspects bomb damage to a German city in 1944.

firestorm uprooted trees and flung cars about like toys. The searing winds set asphalt streets afire. More than 50,000 people died.

In the early stages of the war, British and American air forces suffered heavy losses. In a bombing raid on October 14, 1943, 291 Flying Fortresses set out from Great Britain. Once over Europe, the formation was attacked by wave after wave of German fighters. Sixty bombers were shot down, 138 were damaged.

Early in 1944, Americans began using a long-range fighter, the P-51 Mustang, to escort heavy bombers to and from their targets. The Mustang helped cut losses.

In the final year of the war in Europe, Allied bombers concentrated on key tar-gets. In August 1944, for example, American bombers struck the oilfields of Ploesti, Romania, which provided one third of Germany's petroleum needs. The raid dealt Hitler's war machine a heavy blow.

The Ruhr Valley, where much of Germany's war industry was concentrated, was battered over and over. The nation's roads and railways were put in ruins. Steel production was knocked out. Power plants were leveled. City after city was laid to waste.

Some military leaders said they could bomb Germany out of the war. They were wrong. But night-and-day bombing of Germany helped to destroy the nation's industrial might, and thus played a vital role in the eventual defeat of the Axis.

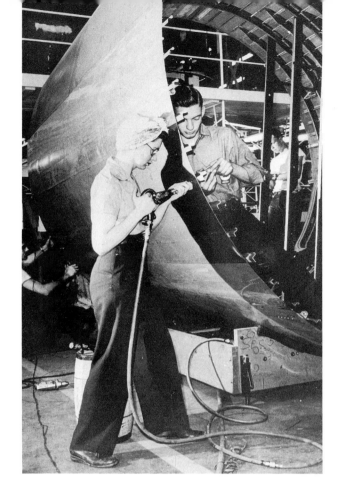

Women by the millions took jobs in war plants, shipyards, and aircraft factories.

On the Home Front

Within weeks after the bombing of Pearl Harbor, virtually every American became caught up in the effort to win the war. Millions went to work in plants that produced war goods. People on the home front bought war bonds and paid taxes to help finance the war.

Children helped out. They collected scrap metal and waste paper to be used in the manufacture of war materials. In Chicago, every Wednesday was "Paper Day," and children carried bundles of discarded newspapers to school for collection. Phonograph records were donated for their wax. Cooking fats went off to war, too.

The role of women changed drastically. In the late 1930s and early 1940s, women who worked outside the home were usu-

Two Girl Scouts sort shoes donated as part of the Victory Clothing Drive.

From 1941–1945, Hollywood movies often had a wartime theme. This one starred Ronald Reagan (center), who would later become the nation's fortieth president.

ally teachers, librarians, secretaries, or sales clerks. But as more and more men went into the armed services, women were called upon to take their places in war plants and shipyards. By 1943, more than five million American women were at work in war industries.

Women also began to take jobs previously held only by men. Women became gas station attendants, cab drivers, and letter carriers.

America was also drastically changed by the mass movement of southern blacks who had left their homes to take jobs in war plants in northern cities.

Although most manufacturing plants were operating on an around-the-clock basis and workers were earning higher wages than ever before, people's purchases were limited. A new car, for example, was out of the question. Automobile manufacturers stopped making cars in 1942 in order to produce trucks, tanks, jeeps, and other vehicles needed by the military.

Factories that once produced appliances turned out war goods instead. There were no new refrigerators, stoves, radios, alarm

A helmeted air raid warden directs the evacuation of a bus during an air raid drill.

Members of the Mochida family await a bus that is to take them to a Japanese internment camp in the United States.

clocks, flat irons, or vacuum cleaners during World War II.

Many coastal cities practiced blackouts. At night, sirens wailed and home owners and apartment dwellers had to douse all lights. Helmeted air-raid wardens patrolled the streets to be sure no light was left burning behind an uncovered window. In the event of an air raid, a light could serve as a bombing target.

Security measures also affected many Japanese-Americans living in California, Oregon, and Washington. Rumors circulated that Japanese-Americans were agents of the Japanese government. They were said to be signaling Japanese submarines at night and operating secret radio stations.

Early in 1942, the federal government moved 120,000 Japanese-Americans from their homes in California, Oregon, and

Two members of the Women's Army Corps repair radios at an Army base in Harlingen, Texas.

Because many goods are in short supply, shoppers wait in long lines, like this meat line in lower Manhattan in 1943.

Washington to relocation camps in Colorado, Utah, Arkansas, and other states.

In assigning Japanese-Americans to these camps, the federal government completely disregarded their rights as American citizens. No evidence was presented to show the Japanese-Americans were in any way disloyal.

In 1988, Congress passed legislation to give an apology and $20,000 to each of the Japanese-Americans who had been in an internment camp. About one half of the 120,000 interned were still living.

Many consumer goods were in short supply during the war years. Some had to be rationed. Meat, butter, sugar, cooking fats, coffee, canned foods, shoes, and gasoline were among the rationed items.

Each family received a book of ration stamps. Each rationed item was worth a

In late 1943, in an effort to conserve gasoline and tires, school children at the army base in Plattsburgh, New York, take a horse-drawn bus to school.

certain number of stamps. When making a purchase, money alone wasn't enough. One had to present the proper number of stamps as well.

Gasoline was rationed not only to cut down on the use of fuel but also to conserve rubber. (America's supply of rubber had been cut by the Japanese.) Each car owner received a windshield sticker bearing a letter from A to E. An A sticker was issued to those who used their cars mainly for pleasure driving. It permitted the car owner to purchase only three gallons of gasoline a week. An E sticker went to

doctors, police officers, and others to whom driving was essential. It entitled the car owner to an unlimited amount of gasoline.

Since the United States never came under direct attack during World War II, the American people did not endure the terrible hardships suffered by the people of Europe and East Asia. Yet the war touched the lives of every American. And it uprooted millions, giving them their first look at the country and the world. In so doing, the war changed America as no event before or since.

Hours before D-Day landings, General Eisenhower speaks with paratroops before they board the planes for the assault on continental Europe.

D-Day

June 6, 1944. At a signal given by General Dwight D. Eisenhower, the largest fighting force the world had ever seen swarmed from England across the channel to the beaches of Normandy in France, just east of the Cherbourg Peninsula.

Preparations for the assault had begun as early as 1942. The invasion plan was given the code name "Operation Overlord." Military leaders believed that once Allied armies were ashore in Europe, Germany would be quickly crushed.

The invasion was filled with peril. The enemy had occupied France for four years, so there had been plenty of time to fortify the coast — build gun emplacements, cover the beaches with obstacles, and sow offshore waters with mines. Hitler called the defense system the "Atlantic Wall."

American assault troops land at Omaha Beach.

BE ALERT
ALL MINES AND BOOBY TRAPS
HAVE NOT BEEN CLEARED
WATCH YOUR STEP
YOUR FIRST MISTAKE WILL BE YOUR LAST
DANGER   MINES

As Allied troops advance beyond the invasion beaches, keeping alert could be a matter of life and death.

The Allies, however, dominated the sky. Allied planes pounded enemy defenses and destroyed many of the roads and bridges the Germans planned on using to bring up reserve forces.

D-Day was not easy. The German forces bitterly resisted the landings. At one beach, code-named "Omaha," the swarms

"All the News That's Fit to Print"

The New York Times.

Copyright, 1944, by The New York Times Company.

6 A. M. EXTRA

Partly cloudy and warmer today; moderate to fresh winds.
Temperatures Yesterday—Max., 67; Min., 51
Sunrise, 5:25 A. M.; Sunset, 8:24 P. M.

VOL. XCIII. No. 31,545. Entered as Second-Class Matter, Postoffice, New York, N. Y. NEW YORK, TUESDAY, JUNE 6, 1944. THREE CENTS IN NEW YORK CITY

ALLIED ARMIES LAND IN FRANCE IN THE HAVRE-CHERBOURG AREA; GREAT INVASION IS UNDER WAY

ROOSEVELT SPEAKS

Says Rome's Fall Marks 'One Up and Two to Go' Among Axis Capitals

WARNS WAY IS HARD

Asks World to Give the Italians a Chance for Recovery

The text of President Roosevelt's address is on Page 5.

By CHARLES HURD

Special to THE NEW YORK TIMES.

WASHINGTON, June 5—President Roosevelt hailed tonight the capture of Rome, first of the three major Axis capitals to fall, as a great achievement on the road toward total conquest of the Axis. Rome, he said, marked "one up and two to go."

The President spoke for a quarter-hour on the radio, as had been announced yesterday, but his speech was notable for its lack of heroics. It was in no sense a speech of triumph, but rather a tribute to the United Nations forces and leadership that drove the Germans from Rome.

With this tribute he combined a solemn warning that much greater fighting lies ahead before the Axis is defeated, as well as high tributes to the Italian people, whom he again welcomed as a people into the family of nations opposed to the Axis.

"Italy should go on," Mr. Roosevelt said, "as a great mother nation, contributing to the culture and the progress and the good-will of mankind, developing her special talents in the arts, crafts, and sciences, and preserving her historic and cultural heritage for the benefit of all peoples.

"We want and expect the help of the future Italy toward lasting peace. All the other nations opposed to fascism and nazism ought to help to give Italy a chance."

Shrines Should Live, He Says

President Roosevelt saw considerable significance in the fact that Rome should be the first Axis capital to fall. He remarked its shrines "visible symbols of the faith and determination of the early saints and martyrs that Christianity should live and become universal," and added that "it will be a source of deep satisfaction that the freedom of the Pope and of Vatican City is assured by the armies of the United Nations."

There is significance, too, he added, in the fact that Rome was liberated by a composite force of soldiers from many nations.

Reviewing the military picture, the President pointed out that "it would be unwise to inflate in our own minds the military importance of the capture of Rome." He cautioned his auditors that while the Germans have retreated "thousands of miles" across Africa and back through Italy "they have suffered heavy losses, but not great enough yet to cause collapse."

"Therefore," he added, "the victory still lies some distance ahead. That distance will be covered in due time—have no fear of that. But it will be tough and it will be costly."

Turning to the relief problem in the newly liberated portion of Italy, Mr. Roosevelt noted that some persons thought of the financial cost, but he maintained that the work would pay dividends "by eliminating fascism" and any future desire by Italians to "start another war of aggression." Relief has been planned, he added, but transport demands are so great that "improvement must be gradual."

He warned Italy that it "cannot grow in stature by seeking to build up a great militaristic empire."

Continued on Page 5

Conferees Accept Cabaret Tax Cut

By The Associated Press.

WASHINGTON, June 5—A House-Senate conference committee agreed today to cut back the cabaret tax from 30 to 20 per cent, but eliminated a provision exempting service men and women from the levy.

The group decided to put the national debt limit at $260,000,000,000 as originally requested by the Administration.

The action is subject to House and Senate votes. The conferees met informally today, but members said that the decisions probably would stand as their final recommendation.

The House, at the insistence of a group of Republicans, passed a bill raising the debt ceiling only from $210,000,000,000 to $240,000,000,000. The Senate then put the figure at $260,000,000,000 and attached a rider reducing the cabaret tax from 30 to 20 per cent and exempting men and women in uniform from paying the tax on their checks.

Some tax experts argued that this exemption would make administration of the excise on night clubs impossible.

FEDERAL LAW HELD RULING INSURANCE

Supreme Court, 4-3, Decides Business Is Interstate and Subject to Trust Act

Special to THE NEW YORK TIMES.

WASHINGTON, June 5—The Supreme Court, by a four-to-three decision today, held that the insurance companies of the country, with assets of $37,000,000,000 and annual premium collections in excess of $6,000,000,000, are in interstate commerce and thus subject to the Sherman Anti-Trust Law.

The decision upset precedents which began with a contrary decision by the court more than seventy-five years ago and have been reaffirmed repeatedly since the adoption of the anti-trust law in 1890.

The majority decision, written

Continued on Page 13

PURSUIT ON IN ITALY

Allies Pass Rome, Cross Tiber as Foe Quits Bank Below City

PLANES JOIN IN CHASE

1,200 Vehicles Wrecked—Eighth Army Battles Into More Towns

By The Associated Press.

ROME, June 5—The Allies' armor and motorized infantry roared through Rome today without pausing, crossed the Tiber River and proceeded with the grim task of destroying two battered German armies fleeing to the north.

Fighter-bombers spearheaded the pursuit, jamming the escape highways with burning enemy transport and littering the fields with dead and wounded Germans. The enemy was tired, disorganized and bewildered by the slashing assault, which in twenty-five days had inflicted a major catastrophe on the Germans and liberated Rome almost without damage.

Railway Yards Bombed

Five hundred American heavy bombers blasted railway yards at five points in northern Italy between Venice and Rimini along which the Germans might attempt to move reinforcements and equipment to bolster their beaten armies. Hour after hour, the Allies' planes swept down on highways leading northward and tore the fleeing enemy apart. Twelve hundred combat vehicles were destroyed from dawn to dark yesterday, and hundreds more today. Farther north, medium bombers smashed bridges and rail facilities.

[The Germans have abandoned the entire left bank of the Tiber from Ostia, at its mouth, to Rome, according to a Vichy broadcast quoted by The Associated Press.

[The Germans are already entrenched in mountain positions

Continued on Page 2

War News Summarized

TUESDAY, JUNE 6, 1944

The invasion of western Europe began this morning.

General Eisenhower, in his first communiqué from Supreme Headquarters, Allied Expeditionary Force, issued at 3:30 A. M., said that "Allied naval forces supported by strong air forces began landing Allied armies this morning on the northern coast of France."

The assault was made by British, American and Canadian troops who, under command of Gen. Sir Bernard L. Montgomery, landed in Normandy. London gave no further details but earlier Berlin had broadcast that parachute troops had landed on the Normandy Peninsula near Cherbourg and that invasion forces were pouring from landing craft under cover of warships near Havre. Dunkerque and Calais were being heavily bombed, the Germans said.

Later announcements from Berlin said that there was fighting between Caen and Trouville and that shock troops had swung into action to halt the invasion. [All the foregoing, 1:8.]

General Eisenhower, in an order of the day to each member of the "great crusade," told his men the enemy would fight savagely and added: "We will accept nothing less than full victory. Good luck." In a broadcast to the "Peoples of Western Europe," he said the day would come when he would need their full help. A special word to France added that Frenchmen would rule the country. [1:6-7.] Almost simultaneously it was announced that General de Gaulle had arrived in London. [6:2.]

The liberation of Rome in no way slowed the Allied pursuit of the tired and disorganized German armies in Italy yesterday. Armored and motorized units sped across the Tiber River to press hard upon the retreating enemy's heels. Five hundred heavy bombers joined with lighter aircraft to smash rail and road routes leading to northern Italy and to add to the foe's demoralization. The Eighth Army, despite heavy opposition, especially northeast of Valmontone, captured a number of strategic towns. [1:3; map P. 2.]

General Clark said that parts of the two German armies had been smashed. He doubted the ability of the German Fourteenth to put up effective opposition and declared that the Tenth had taken a bad beating. [3:1.]

King Victor Emmanuel fulfilled his promise and turned over all authority to his son, Crown Prince Humbert. [1:5-6.]

President Roosevelt warned the people of the United States in a radio talk last night not to over-emphasize the military significance of the liberation of Rome. "Germany has not yet been driven to surrender," he said. "Victory still lies some distance ahead. * * * It will be tough and it will be costly." The President appealed to the world to give Italy a chance to contribute her share to a lasting peace. [1:1.]

In the Pacific theatre Americans were converging on the Biak airfields. Allied planes sank one and damaged two Japanese destroyers and shot down at least eighteen aircraft. [8:1.]

FIRST ALLIED LANDING MADE ON SHORES OF WESTERN EUROPE

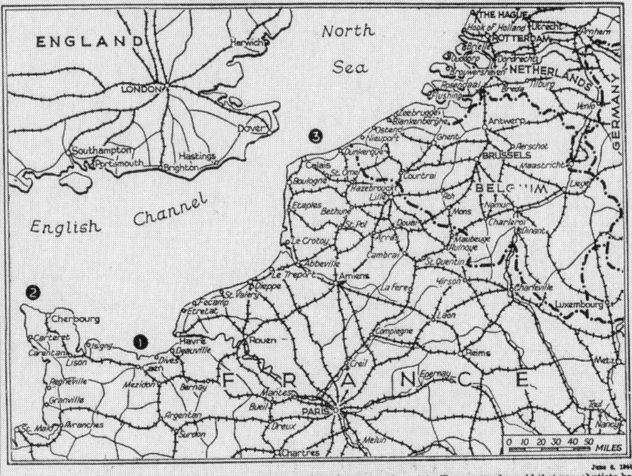

June 6, 1944

General Eisenhower's armies invaded northern France this morning. While the landing points were not specified, the Germans said that troops had gone ashore near Havre and that fighting raged at Caen (1). The enemy also said that parachutists had descended at the northern tip of the Normandy Peninsula (2) and heavy bombing had been visited on Calais and Dunkerque (3).

POPE GIVES THANKS ROME WAS SPARED

Voices Appreciation to Both Belligerents in Message to Throng at St. Peter's

By Wireless to THE NEW YORK TIMES.

VATICAN CITY, June 5—Pope Pius XII appeared on the balcony of St. Peter's at 6 P. M. today to thank God that Rome had been spared from the ravages of war while before him in the densely packed square of St. Peter's and the new broad Via Della Conciliazione tens of thousands of Romans cheered themselves hoarse.

It was the third time today that the Pontiff had showed himself to cheering crowds, as he had appeared twice at a window of his office this morning. But this was a solemn, sacred occasion and no one knowing anything about Pius XII can doubt the fervor of his thankfulness that Rome had been saved.

The Pontiff seemed strong and well and his voice carried far, though it was difficult to hear every word he said because of the crowd.

"We must give thanks to God for the favors we have received," said the Pope. "Rome has been spared. This day will go down in the annals of Rome."

He went on to say he hoped that Italians would be worthy of the grace shown them and put aside hatred and all personal vendettas. He then thanked both belligerents—the Allies and Germany—for having left Rome intact.

After a prayer of thankfulness to the Blessed Virgin and Saints Peter and Paul, guardians of Rome, the Pontiff gave his blessing, "urbe et orbis," as the immense crowd knelt before him.

[The Associated Press estimated the crowd was between 250,000 and 500,000.]

The world has changed for Rome but the Vatican goes on imperturbably as it has through so many other conquests in centuries gone by. It is neutral in fact and spirit. The Pope and all high officials went about their daily routine today as in the past. Except for the tanks and armored cars running along the street in front of St. Peter's one could never know what had happened today.

Continued on Page 5

Italy's Monarch Yields Rule To Son, but Retains Throne

By The Associated Press.

NAPLES, June 5—Victor Emmanuel III stepped aside as King of Italy today, as he previously had said he would do upon the liberation of Rome, and handed to his 39-year-old son, Crown Prince Humbert, all "royal prerogatives." Italian political pressure had been brought to bear against him since the occupation of Naples.

In a decree signed by himself and countersigned by Premier Pietro Badoglio, head of the Italian Liberation Government, the King named his son Lieutenant General of the Realm. The monarch, however, retained his title as head of the House of Savoy and remains as King without power.

[The first act of the Council of Ministers after the transfer of royal powers was a formal denunciation of the 1940 armistice treaty inflicted on France, The United Press said.]

Victor Emmanuel, who became King July 29, 1900, had announced last April 12 his "irrevocable" decision to withdraw from public life "on the day on which Allied troops enter Rome."

Little more than a figurehead since Benito Mussolini assumed the dictatorship of Italy, Victor Emmanuel had won a reputation in the first years of his reign as a sympathetic monarch, interested in his people and their problems.

Prince Humbert, tall and erect, opposed fascism in Italy at the start, but later made a truce with Mussolini. In effect, Humbert becomes the King's regent.

TEXT OF ROYAL DECREE

The King's withdrawal decree:

I, Victor Emmanuel III, by the grace of God and by the will of the nation King of Italy, in collaboration with the President of the Council of Ministers and with the agreement of the Council, have ordered and order as follows:

My beloved son, Humbert of Savoy, Prince of Piedmont, is nominated our Lieutenant General. In collaboration with responsible Ministers he will in our name superintend all matters of administration and exercise all royal prerogatives without exception, signing royal decrees which will be countersigned and authenticated in the usual way.

We order all concerned to observe this decree and to see that it is observed as the law of the State.

Given at Ravello June 5, 1944.
VICTOR EMMANUEL.
(Countersigned) PIETRO BADOGLIO.

The withdrawal was presented to

Continued on Page 4

ALLIED WARNING FLASHED TO COAST

People Told to Clear Area 27 Miles Inland as Soon as Instructions Are Given

By Cable to THE NEW YORK TIMES.

LONDON, Tuesday, June 6—The British Broadcasting Corporation began its 8 A. M. news bulletin this morning with quotations from a Supreme Headquarters' "urgent warning" to inhabitants of the enemy-occupied countries living near the coast.

Gen. Dwight D. Eisenhower has directed that whenever possible in France a warning shall be given to towns in which certain targets will be intensively bombed.

This warning, the broadcast said,

Continued on Page B

PARADE OF PLANES CARRIES INVADERS

Witness Says First 'Chutists Met Only Light Fire When They Landed in France

The first eyewitness account of the Allies' invasion of Europe was given in a pool broadcast from London this morning by Wright Bryan of the National Broadcasting Company, who accompanied the airborne troops in their landings.

His account said the first spearhead of Allied forces landed by parachute in northern France in the first hour of D-day.

"In the navigator's dome in the flight deck of a C-47, I rode across the English Channel with the first group of planes from the United States Ninth Air Force Troop Carrier Command to take our fighting men into Europe," Mr. Bryan said.

He added that just before he left French soil for the return trip he saw seventeen American paratroopers, led by a lieutenant colonel, jump with their arms, ammunition and equipment into German-occupied France."

He declared that his group at the head of the leading wing was met with "only scattering small

Continued on Page B

Eisenhower Instructs Europeans; Gives Battle Order to His Armies

Following are the texts of a statement by Gen. Dwight D. Eisenhower broadcast to the people of western Europe and his Order of the Day to the Allied Expeditionary Force as recorded by The New York Times and the Columbia Broadcasting System:

People of western Europe! A landing was made this morning on the coast of France by troops of the Allied Expeditionary Force. This landing is part of the concerted United Nations plan for the liberation of Europe, made in conjunction with our great Russian Allies. I have this message for all of you. Although the initial assault may not have been made in your own country, the hour of your liberation is approaching.

All patriots, men and women, young and old, have a part to play in the achievement of final victory. To members of resistance movements, whether led by national or outside leaders, I say: "Follow the instructions you have received." To patriots who are not members of organized resistance groups I say, "continue your passive resistance, but do not needlessly endanger your lives until I give you the signal to rise and strike the enemy. The day will come when I shall need your united strength. Until that day, I call on you for the hard task of discipline and restraint."

Citizens of France! I am proud to have again under my command the gallant forces of France. Fighting beside their Allies, they will play a worthy part in the liberation of their

Continued on Page 3

EISENHOWER ACTS

U. S., British, Canadian Troops Backed by Sea, Air Forces

MONTGOMERY LEADS

Nazis Say Their Shock Units Are Battling Our Parachutists

Communique No. 1 On Allied Invasion

By Broadcast to THE NEW YORK TIMES.

LONDON, Tuesday, June 6—The Supreme Headquarters of the Allied Expeditionary Force issued this communiqué this morning:

"Under the command of General Eisenhower, Allied naval forces, supported by strong air forces, began landing Allied armies this morning on the northern coast of France."

By RAYMOND DANIELL

By Cable to THE NEW YORK TIMES.

SUPREME HEADQUARTERS ALLIED EXPEDITIONARY FORCES, Tuesday, June 6—The invasion of Europe from the west has begun.

In the gray light of a summer dawn Gen. Dwight D. Eisenhower threw his great Anglo-American force into action today for the liberation of the Continent. The spearhead of attack was an Army group commanded by Gen. Sir Bernard L. Montgomery and comprising troops of the United States, Britain and Canada.

General Eisenhower's first communiqué was terse and calculated to give little information to the enemy. It said merely that "Allied naval forces supported by strong air forces began landing Allied armies this morning on the northern coast of France."

After the first communiqué was released it was announced that the Allied landing was in Normandy.

Caen Battle Reported

German broadcasts, beginning at 6:30 A. M., London time, [12:30 A. M. Eastern war time] gave first word of the assault. [The Associated Press said General Eisenhower, for the sake of surprise, deliberately let the Germans have the "first word."]

The German DNB agency said the Allied invasion operations began with the landing of airborne troops in the area of the mouth of the Seine River.

[Berlin said the "center of gravity" of the fierce fighting was at Caen, thirty miles southwest of Havre and sixty-five miles southeast of Cherbourg, The Associated Press reported. Caen is ten miles inland from the sea, at the base of the seventy-five-mile-wide Normandy Peninsula, and fighting there might indicate the Allies' seizing of a beachhead.

[DNB said in a broadcast just before 10 A. M. (4 A. M. Eastern war time) that the Anglo-American troops had been reinforced at dawn at the mouth of the Seine River in the Havre area.]

[An Allied correspondent broadcasting from Supreme Headquarters, according to the Columbia Broadcasting System, said this morning that "German tanks are moving up

Continued on Page A Following Page 3

Troops in Normandy in charge of supplies.

Coast Guardsman Charles W. Tyner examines the jagged shrapnel hole in the helmet he wore during the initial assault on the beaches of Southern France. Unbelievably, Tyner suffered just a superficial scratch.

of landing craft filled with wet, cold, and nervous soldiers came under murderous machine-gun and artillery fire. Some of the boats were sunk before they reached the beach. Wounded men drowned in shallow water. For hours, the troops on Omaha beach struggled to survive.

Many ships came in close to shell the enemy strong points. Tanks and heavy artillery were brought ashore. Slowly, the picture began to change.

In the first 24 hours, thousands of men died or were wounded. Despite the losses, Allied forces managed to secure several shaky beachheads on the Normandy shore.

Then the struggle began to widen the beachheads. Normandy's winding roads and open fields enclosed by thick hedgerows favored the enemy. Nevertheless,

American paratroopers, among the first to make successful landings on the continent, hold a Nazi flag captured in a village assault.

within two months after D-Day, two million Allied troops were ashore in France.

In mid-August, two Allied armies — one American, the other French — landed in southern France near the town of Nice. They drove north to join Allied forces that had broken out of the Normandy beachhead. Then, on a wide front, the Allies began a steady advance toward Germany's heart.

Today, along Normandy's channel coast, there are many grim reminders of D-Day. Massive German guns anchored in concrete look down on the shoreline. Rusting hulks of ships that formed the invasion armada jut out of the sea. And not far from the beaches, in quiet military cemeteries, stand neat rows of white crosses and Stars of David. They document the real cost of D-Day.

American troops move through the French town of Carentan.

The Battle of the Bulge

"To attack is the best defense" is a well-known piece of military strategy. Late in 1944, Hitler decided to test this theory.

That summer, Allied armies had pushed out of Normandy to retake most of France and Belgium and advance into Holland and Germany itself. They paused before reaching the Rhine River, which flows through western Germany and the Netherlands to empty into the North Sea.

Unknown to the Allies, Hitler was planning a last-stand counteroffensive by which he hoped to recapture the Belgian seaport of Antwerp and split the Allied

Loaded down with full packs, American soldiers are greeted by General Eisenhower as they march to a train that is to carry them to a reinforcement camp.

American prisoners of war after being captured by the Germans during the Battle of the Bulge.

armies. On December 16 under the cover of fog, German forces launched their attack. The Allies were confused at first and slow to react. While the Allied line held on flanks, in the center the Germans burst through, overrunning Allied positions. (The German breakthrough created a bulging shape on the map, which led it to be called the Battle of the Bulge.)

About a week after the attack began, the weather cleared and Allied aircraft took to the air in support of ground troops. Allied forces regrouped and counterattacked. By early January 1945, the Allies regained all the land that had been lost.

The Battle of the Bulge was Hitler's final gamble in defense of Germany's heartland. And it failed.

Joyous French men and women, boys and girls, greet Allied soldiers following the liberation of Paris.

Germany Surrenders

By the early months of 1945, Germany was on the brink of collapse. Allied armies were pressing toward Berlin and the heart of Germany from every direction. The once powerful German air force had suffered devastating losses. There were no more men to draft for the army. Allied bombers had battered Germany's industries. Germany's cities lay in ruins.

Russian troops had succeeded in recapturing the Ukraine and the Crimea. They

When Russian and American forces link up, an American photographer is grabbed by a Russian soldier, who hugs and kisses him, shouting, "Americano, Americano!"

had swept into eastern Poland and Lithuania, into Romania, Bulgaria, eastern Hungary, and Czechoslovakia. For their final drive, the Russians assembled a fighting force of more than four million men.

Meanwhile, in America, President Roosevelt lay sick and dying at Warm Springs, Georgia. He died on April 12, 1945. People from all around the world mourned his passing. Vice President

Harry S Truman became President.

Within two weeks after Roosevelt's death, American patrols joined forces with units from the Soviet Union at Torgau on the Elbe River. Events were moving swiftly. On April 30, Hitler committed suicide by swallowing poison and shooting himself. Aides burned his body with gasoline. In Berlin the next day, Russian soldiers hoisted the Soviet flag atop the ruins

"All the News That's Fit to Print"

The New York Times.

LATE CITY EDITION
Clearing and warm today.
Fair, continued warm tomorrow.
Temperatures Yesterday—Max., 74; Min., 54
Sunrise today, 6:21 A. M.; Sunset, 7:35 P. M.

VOL. XCIV...No. 31,856. Entered as Second-Class Matter, Postoffice, New York, N. Y. NEW YORK, FRIDAY, APRIL 13, 1945. THREE CENTS IN NEW YORK CITY

PRESIDENT ROOSEVELT IS DEAD; TRUMAN TO CONTINUE POLICIES; 9TH CROSSES ELBE, NEARS BERLIN

U. S. AND RED ARMIES DRIVE TO MEET

Americans Across the Elbe in Strength Race Toward Russians Who Have Opened Offensive From Oder

WEIMAR TAKEN, RUHR POCKET SLASHED

Third Army Reported 19 Miles From Czechoslovak Border—British Drive Deeper in the North, Seizing Celle—Canadians Freeing Holland

By DREW MIDDLETON
By Wireless to THE NEW YORK TIMES.

PARIS, April 12—Thousands of tanks and a half million doughboys of the United States First, Third and Ninth Armies are racing through the heart of the Reich on a front of 150 miles, threatening Berlin, Leipzig and the last citadels of the Nazi power.

The Second Armored Division of the Ninth Army has crossed the Elbe River in force and is striking eastward toward Berlin, whose outskirts lie less than sixty miles to the east, according to reports from the front. [A report quoted by The United Press placed the Americans less than fifty miles from the capital.] Beyond Berlin the First White Russian Army has crossed the Oder on a wide front and a junction between the western and eastern Allies is not far off.

[The Moscow radio reported that heavy battles were raging west of the Oder before Berlin, indicating that Marshal Gregory K. Zhukoff had launched his drive toward the Reich's capital. The Soviet communiqué announced further progress by the Red Army forces in and around Vienna.]

Paris is wild with excitement tonight. A special edition of the newspaper France-Soir carries a report by the radio station "Voice of America" that places American forces fifteen and five-eighths miles from Berlin after an airborne landing that had linked up with Lieut. Gen. William H. Simpson's forces advancing eastward from the Elbe. This would put American forces only seventy-five miles from the Red Army vanguard.

No Confirmation at Headquarters

There was no confirmation of this report at Allied Supreme Headquarters, which by its own admission was thirty-six hours behind developments on some sectors of the front.

Resistance was continuing only on the northern and southern flanks. The center had burst wide open. Weimar fell to Lieut. Gen. George S. Patton's infantry, and reports from the front said Erfurt also had been cleared. Schweinfurt and Heilbronn, two German bastions on the south, had fallen to United States Seventh Army forces, who were driving on Bamberg, while farther north Third Army forces were about thirty-five miles from the Czechoslovak frontier in the area east of Coburg.

[The German radio reported American Third Army forces at Lichtenberg, nineteen miles from the Czechoslovak border, The United Press said.]

The offensives to liberate the Netherlands and reduce the Ruhr

Continued on Page 12, Column 2

OUR OKINAWA GUNS DOWN 118 PLANES

Japanese Fliers Start 'Suicide' Attacks on Fleet, Sink a Destroyer, Hit Other Ships

By W. H. LAWRENCE
By Wireless to THE NEW YORK TIMES.

GUAM, Friday, April 13—Japanese attempting to halt the American march to Tokyo, have started "desperate, suicidal" aerial attacks upon our ships and men in the Okinawa area, losing 118 planes on Thursday alone, Fleet Admiral Chester W. Nimitz announced today.

The Japanese succeeded in sinking a destroyer and damaging several other surface units, the communiqué said. All of the damaged vessels remained in action.

It was the first time that the Navy had revealed the suicidal nature of the Japanese air missions against our ships and men. The Japanese radio has been saying that this type of assault was being carried on by a "special attack corps" known in Japanese as "kamakazi," which, translated literally, means "divine wind."

Attack at Low Levels

The Japanese fliers launched their attacks upon our ships and men at a high speed and from low levels, diving directly into a ship or troop concentration to explode their bombs as they crashed.

There was no official estimate of the total number of enemy aircraft engaged in the Okinawa area attack other than the report of the 118 enemy planes destroyed.

Admiral Nimitz reported that the attacks began early on April 12 (Eastern Longitude time) with seven enemy planes shot down during the morning in the vicinity of the Hagushi beaches.

The tempo of the attack was stepped up in the afternoon as the Japanese bore in on our ships in wave after wave. Admiral Nimitz said that ships' guns, carrier aircraft and shore-based anti-aircraft shot down 111 of the attackers.

The revelation of the suicidal Japanese air attacks was the highlight of Admiral Nimitz' regular morning communiqué, which also disclosed the identity of two Marine and two Army divisions that have gone into action on Okinawa. These included the Twenty-seventh Army Division, formed from New York National Guard units, which are seeing action for the first time since the Saipan campaign and previously had engaged in the Gilbert Islands assault. It is com-

Continued on Page 18, Column 3

Army Leaders See Reich End at Hand

By The Associated Press.

WASHINGTON, April 12—High Army officials told Senators today that the end of organized fighting in Germany probably would come within a few days.

Describing the pell-mell dash of American Armies across Germany, General Staff officers expressed the opinion to members of the Senate Military Committee that a collapse of German arms was imminent.

Those who attended said the army chiefs declared that they were so sure of the results that orders had been drawn for a drastic reduction in shipments of durable equipment to Europe.

Franklin Delano Roosevelt
1882-1945

SECURITY PARLEY WON'T BE DELAYED

State Department Urges That World Be Shown We Plan No Changes in Policy

By JAMES B. RESTON
Special to THE NEW YORK TIMES.

WASHINGTON, April 12—The United Nations Security Conference will open in San Francisco on April 25, despite the death of President Roosevelt, Secretary of State Edward R. Stettinius Jr. announced tonight.

Mr. Stettinius said that he had been authorized by President Harry Truman to make this announcement after a meeting of the Cabinet at the White House.

Most of the overseas delegations to the San Francisco conference have either arrived in this country or are now on their way, but while this was said to have been a factor in the decision to proceed with the conference, State Department officials urged that every attempt be made to give immediate evidence to the world that President Roosevelt's foreign policy would be sustained by the new Administration.

President Roosevelt had planned to address the San Francisco conference. His interest in an international organization of nations to maintain peace and security had gone back to his service in the Wilson Administration, when he sat in the gallery of the Senate and listened to the debate that resulted in the rejection of the League of Nations Covenant. He had expressed to friends his desire to participate in the San Francisco conference and to see the United States enter the new League during his term in office.

The sudden elevation of Presi-

Continued on Page 3, Column 1

War News Summarized

FRIDAY, APRIL 13, 1945

President Roosevelt died yesterday afternoon, suddenly and unexpectedly. He was stricken with a massive cerebral hemorrhage at Warm Springs, Ga., on the eve of his greatest military and diplomatic successes—the impending fall of Berlin and the opening of the San Francisco Conference to set up a World Security Organization that would make the world free from martial and economic strife [1:7-8.]

Mr. Roosevelt had been sitting in front of the fireplace of his Little White House, having gone to Warm Springs on March 30 for a three-week rest. About 2:15 Eastern war time he said, "I have a terrific headache," lost consciousness in a few moments and died at 4:35. He was 63 years old. [1:6.]

The tragic word spread quickly around the world. Expressions of sorrow poured in from all sections. [4:5.] American soldiers and sailors refused to believe the reports until there was no longer doubt that their Commander in Chief had gone. [4:2-3.]

Harry S. Truman was sworn in as President at 7:09 o'clock last night, and a few minutes later Mrs. Roosevelt left for Warm Springs. [1:7.] The new President immediately called a Cabinet meeting and declared that Mr. Roosevelt's policies would be continued, that the war would be carried on until Germany and Japan surrendered unconditionally and that the San Francisco Conference would open April 25 as scheduled. [1:3.]

Some 500,000 American soldiers of the Third and Ninth Armies, and thousands of tanks, sped along a 150-mile front toward Berlin and Leipzig. The Ninth, surging across the Elbe, according to delayed reports was less than fifty miles from the German capital and 115 from the Russians along the Oder. The Third Army captured Weimar, home of the late German Republic, and was twenty-three miles below Leipzig, with the First closing a pincers from the north. [1:1-2; map P. 2.]

The Moscow radio reported that the Red Army was waging fierce battles east of Berlin, indicating resumption of the drive on that city. Elsewhere Russian troops scored wide gains and cut the last escape railroad from Vienna. [13:1.]

Open cities were ruled out and every German was ordered by Himmler to fight to the death, although Goebbels said "the war cannot last much longer." [12:6-7.]

The Ninth Air Force destroyed at least 117 more German planes yesterday. [11:8.]

In Italy the Eighth Army advanced along a thirty-mile front toward Bologna and the Po Valley; the Fifth Army also made good gains and was eleven miles from La Spezia. [13:8, with map.]

Japanese planes resumed their suicide attacks on American ships off Okinawa, sinking a destroyer and damaging several other vessels. One hundred and eighteen enemy planes were shot down. [1:2.] The Americal Division invaded Bohol, last of the enemy-held central Philippines. [18:6.] The B-29 attack on Koriyama, 110 miles north of Tokyo, set a new Superfortress distance record. [18:2.]

Secretary of State Stettinius and Secretary of War Stimson, denouncing Germany's "steadily increasing" mistreatment of American prisoners, said those responsible would be brought to justice. [13:6-7.]

Clashes between Right and Left wing elements in Iran were reported from Moscow. [13:2.]

LAST WORDS: 'I HAVE TERRIFIC HEADACHE'

Roosevelt Was Posing for Artist When Hemorrhage Struck—He Died in Bedroom

By The Associated Press.

WARM SPRINGS, Ga., April 12—President Franklin D. Roosevelt's last words were:

"I have a terrific headache."

He spoke them to Comdr. Howard G. Bruenn, naval physician.

Mr. Roosevelt was sitting in front of a fireplace in the Little White House here atop Pine Mountain when what was described as a massive cerebral hemorrhage struck him.

The President's Negro valet, Arthur Prettyman, and a Filipino messboy carried him to his bedroom. He was unconscious at the end. It came without pain.

Dr. Bruenn said that he saw the President this morning and he was in excellent spirits at 9:30 A. M.

"At 1 o'clock," Dr. Bruenn added, "he was sitting in a chair while sketches were being made of him by an artist. He suddenly complained of a very severe occipital headache (back of the head).

"Within a very few minutes he lost consciousness. He was seen by me at 1:30 P. M., fifteen minutes after the episode had started.

"He did not regain consciousness, and he died at 3:35 P. M. (Georgia time)."

The artist sketching Mr. Roosevelt was N. Robbins of 520 West 139th Street, New York.

Only others present in the cottage were Comdr. George Fox, White House pharmacist and long an attendant on the President; William D. Hassett, Presidential secretary; Miss Grace Tully, con-

Continued on Page 4, Column 2

END COMES SUDDENLY AT WARM SPRINGS

Even His Family Unaware of Condition as Cerebral Stroke Brings Death to Nation's Leader at 63

ALL CABINET MEMBERS TO KEEP POSTS

Funeral to Be at White House Tomorrow, With Burial at Hyde Park Home—Impact of News Tremendous

By ARTHUR KROCK
Special to THE NEW YORK TIMES.

WASHINGTON, April 12—Franklin Delano Roosevelt, War President of the United States and the only Chief Executive in history who was chosen for more than two terms, died suddenly and unexpectedly at 4:35 P. M. today at Warm Springs, Ga., and the White House announced his death at 5:48 o'clock. He was 63.

The President, stricken by a cerebral hemorrhage, passed from unconsciousness to death on the eighty-third day of his fourth term and in an hour of high triumph. The armies and fleets under his direction as Commander in Chief were at the gates of Berlin and the shores of Japan's home islands as Mr. Roosevelt died, and the cause he represented and led was nearing the conclusive phase of success.

Less than two hours after the official announcement, Harry S. Truman of Missouri, the Vice President, took the oath as the thirty-second President. The oath was administered by the Chief Justice of the United States, Harlan F. Stone, in a one-minute ceremony at the White House. Mr. Truman immediately let it be known that Mr. Roosevelt's Cabinet is remaining in office at his request, and that he had authorized Secretary of State Edward R. Stettinius Jr. to proceed with plans for the United Nations Conference on international organization at San Francisco, scheduled to begin April 25. A report was circulated that he leans somewhat to the idea of a coalition Cabinet, but this is unsubstantiated.

Funeral Tomorrow Afternoon

It was disclosed by the White House that funeral services for Mr. Roosevelt would take place at 4 P. M. (E. W. T.) Saturday in the East Room of the Executive Mansion. The Rev. Angus Dun, Episcopal Bishop of Washington; the Rev. Howard S. Wilkinson of St. Thomas's Church in Washington and the Rev. John G. McGee of St. John's in Washington will conduct the services.

The body will be interred at Hyde Park, N. Y., Sunday, with the Rev. George W. Anthony of St. James Church officiating. The time has not yet been fixed.

Jonathan Daniels, White House secretary, said Mr. Roosevelt's body would not lie in state. He added that, in view of the limited size of the East Room, which holds only about 200 persons, the list of those attending the funeral services would be limited to high Government officials, representatives of the membership of both

Continued on Page 3, Column 2

TRUMAN IS SWORN IN THE WHITE HOUSE

Members of Cabinet on Hand as Chief Justice Stone Administers the Oath

By C. P. TRUSSELL
Special to THE NEW YORK TIMES.

WASHINGTON, April 12—Vice President Harry S. Truman of Missouri, standing erect, with his sharp features taut and looking straight ahead through his large, round glasses, became the thirty-second President of the United States in a ceremony lasting not more than a minute in the Cabinet Room of the White House at 7:09 o'clock tonight.

The oath was administered by Chief Justice Harlan F. Stone two hours and thirty-four minutes after the sudden death of President Roosevelt at Warm Springs. Mr. Truman had picked up a Bible from the end of the big Cabinet conference table, held it with his left hand and placed his right hand upon the upper cover. After repeating the oath, he bowed his head, lifted the Bible to his lips and kissed it.

Even before he had taken the oath Mr. Truman had asked President Roosevelt's Cabinet to continue in service. He also authorized Edward R. Stettinius Jr., Secretary of State, to announce that the United Nations Conference for International Organization would go on as scheduled.

To the newsmen at the White House he sent this word, through Stephen Early, press secretary:

"For the time being I prefer not to hold a press conference. It will be my effort to carry on as I believe the President would have done, and to that end I have asked the Cabinet to stay on with me."

Soon after he became President, Mr. Truman left the White House for the five-room Connecticut Avenue apartment where he has resided with Mrs. Truman and their 20-year-old daughter, Mary Margaret, for four years. He said he was "going home, to bed."

It was shortly after he had finished presiding over the Senate debate on the United States-Mexican Water Treaty late this afternoon that Mr. Truman received word from the White House of President Roosevelt's death. This was at about 5:15 P. M., a half hour before the news was made public. Reaching for his hat, he dashed out of the office, calling back to his staff that he was going to the White House.

Arriving at the White House, the

Continued on Page 3, Column 6

Byrnes May Take Post With Truman

Special to THE NEW YORK TIMES.

WASHINGTON, April 12—James F. Byrnes, recently resigned as Director of War Mobilization and Reconversion, known to be one of President Truman's warmest friends in official Washington, is expected to be called to the White House for consultation, and possibly to take an important post in the Cabinet, in the immediate future.

President Truman's admiration of former Justice Byrnes is well known here. He undoubtedly would have been Mr. Truman's choice as a successor to Cordell Hull as Secretary of State.

New Yorkers celebrate in Times Square upon hearing news of Germany's surrender.

of the Reichstag, the German parliament.

Germany collapsed in chaos. Soldiers deserted from the army. Many Nazi leaders killed themselves. Others sought to escape. Berlin fell to the Russians on May 2, 1945.

Early on the morning of May 7, Colonel General Alfred Jodl, representing the German high command, entered the Allied headquarters in a red school building at Reims, in France. There, on behalf of the German government, Jodl signed the terms of surrender. Lieutenant General Walter Bedell Smith, Chief of Staff for General Eisenhower, signed for the Allies.

President Truman proclaimed the following day, May 8, to be V-E Day — Victory in Europe Day. It had been five years, eight months, and seven days since Hitler's troops had invaded Poland.

"All the News That's Fit to Print"

The New York Times.

LATE CITY EDITION
Cloudy with showers today. Partly cloudy and cooler tomorrow.
Temperature Yesterday—Max., 64; Min., 47
Sunrise today, 5:46 A. M.; Sunset, 7:58 P. M.

Copyright, 1945, by The New York Times Company

VOL. XCIV..No. 31,881.

Entered as Second-Class Matter, Postoffice, New York, N. Y.

NEW YORK, TUESDAY, MAY 8, 1945.

THREE CENTS NEW YORK CITY

THE WAR IN EUROPE IS ENDED!
SURRENDER IS UNCONDITIONAL;
V-E WILL BE PROCLAIMED TODAY;
OUR TROOPS ON OKINAWA GAIN

ISLAND-WIDE DRIVE

Marines Reach Village a Mile From Naha and Army Lines Advance

7 MORE SHIPS SUNK

Search Planes Again Hit Japan's Life Line— Kyushu Bombed

By WARREN MOSCOW
By Wireless to The New York Times.

GUAM, Tuesday, May 8—In an island-wide American advance on Okinawa yesterday the First Marine Division drove south to the edge of Dakeshi Village, about a mile from Naha, the capital, straightening out the line on our right flank. In the center the Seventy-seventh Army Division used flame-throwing tanks for considerable advances, while the Seventh Army Division moved forward on the left flank.

[Airfields on Kyushu, southern Japan, were bombed Monday and Tuesday by Superfortresses, two of which were lost in heavy air opposition.

[Allied fliers started operating from the Tarakan airfield although fighting continued on that island of Borneo, and in the Philippines American troops made advances on Mindanao and Luzon.]

Japanese Dead at 36,535

As the United States forces on Okinawa resumed their drive, Fleet Admiral Chester W. Nimitz revealed that Japanese killed on the island had mounted to 36,535 on Monday, showing that the Americans were maintaining their rate of 1,000 a day.

The Americans have not yet taken the main Japanese artillery emplacements on Okinawa, which were the principal targets of the fleet off the island. The fleet's guns continued yesterday, along with carrier aircraft, to support the ground movements.

Meanwhile search bombers of Fleet Air Wing 1 continued to give an impressive demonstration of what the tightening air blockade of Japan will mean. Attacking at mast-head height with bombs and machine guns, these long-range aircraft, based in the Okinawa area, sank four more ships in waters off Korea and damaged five others.

The ships sunk were a large cargo ship, a medium cargo ship, a medium oiler and a large fleet tanker. Two small freighters were

Continued on Page 12, Column 2

Leopold Rescued By 7th Army Troops

WITH THE UNITED STATES SEVENTH ARMY, Tuesday, May 8—Leopold III, King of Belgium, and his wife, Princess Rethy, have been liberated by the Seventh Army, it was announced today.

They were found near Strobl, eight miles east of Salzburg. The Americans had been told of their whereabouts by civilians.

With the King and his wife were eighteen members of their staff and four children. All were in good health.

Elements of the American 106th Cavalry Group had to

The Pulitzer Awards For 1944 Announced

The Pulitzer Prize awards announced yesterday by the trustees of Columbia University included: For a distinguished novel, to "A Bell for Adano," by John Hersey; for an original American play of the current season, to "Harvey," by Mary Chase.

Among the newspaper awards were those to Hal Boyle, Associated Press war reporter, for distinguished correspondence; to James B. Reston of THE NEW YORK TIMES for his reporting of the Dumbarton Oaks Security Conference; to Joe Rosenthal, Associated Press photographer, for his photograph of marines raising the American flag at Iwo; and to The Detroit Free Press for "distinguished and meritorious public service" in its investigation of legislative corruption at Lansing, Mich.

Further details of the awards will be found on Page 16.

MOLOTOFF HAILS BASIC 'UNANIMITY'

He Stresses Five Points In World Charter, but His View on One Is Questioned

By JAMES B. RESTON
Special to The New York Times.

SAN FRANCISCO, May 7—The major issue concerning Germany's unconditional surrender have reached "unanimity" on the kind of world security organization which should be created at the United Nations conference to protect their newly won victory, Vyacheslaff M. Molotoff, Russian Foreign Commissar, said today.

While the delegates at the conference celebrated the end of the European war, and three Foreign Ministers, T. V. Soong of China, Paul Henri Spaak of Belgium and Trygve Lie of Norway left the conference to deal with urgent official business elsewhere, Mr. Molotoff told the press that the Soviet Union attached the "greatest importance" to five agreements reached by the heads of the Big Four delegations.

First, he said, these leaders agreed to support the principles of justice, international law, human rights and fundamental freedom for all.

Second, he added, the Big Four agreed not to make provision in the security charter for the revision of treaties.

His statement on this point was ambiguous and led to some speculation as to the unanimity of all four on the question.

Revision Power Called Danger

A reference in the United Nations charter to the necessity of revising treaties, Mr. Molotoff stated, "would play into the hands of enemy countries, which would certainly like to undermine and emasculate these treaties." Furthermore, he declared, to give the new League of Nations authority to consider revision of treaties would be a violation of national sovereign rights, which are guaranteed in the Dumbarton Oaks Charter.

For these reasons, he concluded, "the idea of revising treaties was rejected as untenable."

Third, Mr. Molotoff said, it was agreed among the Big Four that treaties directed against Germany, such as Russia's twenty-year alliance with Britain, France, Czechoslovakia, Yugoslavia and the War saw Poles, "should remain in force until such time as the Government concerned felt that the interna-

GERMANY SURRENDERS: NEW YORKERS MASSED UNDER SYMBOL OF LIBERTY

Thousands filling Times Square in spontaneous celebration yesterday

The New York Times

PRAGUE SAYS FOES ACCEPT SURRENDER

Czechoslovak Radio Reports All Fighting in Bohemia Will Be Ended Today

By The Associated Press

LONDON, Tuesday, May 8—The Czechoslovak - controlled Prague radio announced today that the Germans in Prague and throughout Bohemia, a last major holdout pocket of German resistance, had accepted unconditional surrender.

The announcement came as the United States Third Army was reported to have advanced to the outskirts of the Czechoslovak capital, and three Russian armies hammered toward the same goal from the east and north.

The German military plenipotentiary is negotiating with the Czechoslovak National Council on the modalities of unconditional surrender," said the broadcast, detailing what purported to be the

Continued on Page 11, Column 2

Wild Crowds Greet News In City While Others Pray

By FRANK S. ADAMS

New York City's millions reacted in two sharply contrasting ways yesterday to the news of the unconditional surrender of the German armies. A large and noisy minority greeted it with the turbulent enthusiasm of New Year's Eve and Election Night rolled into one. However, the great bulk of the city's population responded with quiet thanksgiving that the war in Europe was won, tempered by the realization that a grim and bitter struggle still was ahead in the Pacific and the fact that the nation is still in mourning for the fallen President and Commander in Chief.

Times Square, the financial section and the garment district were thronged from mid-morning on with wildly jubilant celebrators who tooted horns, staged impromptu parades and filled the canyons between the skyscrapers with fluttering scraps of paper. Elsewhere in the metropolitan area, however, war plants continued to hum, schools, offices and

factories carried on their normal activities, and residential areas were calmly joyful.

One factor that helped to dampen the celebration was the bewilderment of large segments of the population at the absence of an official proclamation to back up the news contained in flaring headlines and radio bulletins. With the premature rumor of ten days ago fresh in everyone's mind, and millions still mindful of the false armistice of 1918, there was widespread skepticism over the authenticity of the news.

By mid-afternoon loudspeakers were blaring into the ears of the exulting thousands in the amusement district the news that President Truman's proclamation was being held up by the necessity of coordinating it with the announcements from London and Moscow, and that the formal celebration of the long-awaited V-E Day would be delayed until today.

This sobering note gradually

Continued on Page 7, Column 1

GERMANS CAPITULATE ON ALL FRONTS

American, Russian and French Generals Accept Surrender in Eisenhower Headquarters, a Reims School

REICH CHIEF OF STAFF ASKS FOR MERCY

Doenitz Orders All Military Forces of Germany To Drop Arms—Troops in Norway Give Up —Churchill and Truman on Radio Today

By EDWARD KENNEDY
Associated Press Correspondent

REIMS, France, May 7—Germany surrendered unconditionally to the Western Allies and the Soviet Union at 2:41 A. M. French time today. [This was at 8:41 P. M., Eastern Wartime Sunday.]

The surrender took place at a little red schoolhouse that is the headquarters of Gen. Dwight D. Eisenhower.

The surrender, which brought the war in Europe to a formal end after five years, eight months and six days of bloodshed and destruction, was signed for Germany by Col. Gen. Gustav Jodl. General Jodl is the new Chief of Staff of the German Army.

The surrender was signed for the Supreme Allied Command by Lieut. Gen. Walter Bedell Smith, Chief of Staff for General Eisenhower.

It was also signed by Gen. Ivan Susloparoff for the Soviet Union and by Gen. Francois Sevez for France.

[The official Allied announcement will be made at 9 o'clock Tuesday morning when President Truman will broadcast a statement and Prime Minister Churchill will issue a V-E Day proclamation. Gen. Charles de Gaulle also will address the French at the same time.]

General Eisenhower was not present at the signing, but immediately afterward General Jodl and his fellow delegate, Gen. Admiral Hans Georg Friedeburg, were received by the Supreme Commander.

Germans Say They Understand Terms

They were asked sternly if they understood the surrender terms imposed upon Germany and if they would be carried out by Germany.

They answered Yes.

Germany, which began the war with a ruthless attack upon Poland, followed by successive aggressions and brutality in internment camps, surrendered with an appeal to the victors for mercy toward the German people and armed forces.

After having signed the full surrender, General Jodl said he wanted to speak and received leave to do so.

"With this signature," he said in soft-spoken German, "the German people and armed forces are for better or worse delivered into the victors' hands.

"In this war, which has lasted more than five years, both have achieved and suffered more than perhaps any other people in the world."

SHAEF BAN ON AP LIFTED IN 6 HOURS

Action Comes After Protests From Newspapers and Public —Writer Still Barred

Suspension of filing facilities of The Associated Press in the European theatre was clamped on by Supreme Headquarters, Allied Expeditionary Force (SHAEF), yesterday in an unprecedented action and was lifted six hours and twenty minutes later.

The ban was continued, however, on all copy submitted for clearance by Edward Kennedy, chief of the press association's staff on the Western Front, who sent the momentous story announcing Germany's final surrender in a dispatch from Reims, France, which was received in New York over the AP wires at 9:35 A. M. (EWT).

It was not until seven hours and fifty-five minutes had elapsed after

Continued on Page 4, Column 2

Summary of News of the War and German Surrender

TUESDAY, MAY 8, 1945

The war ended in Europe yesterday after five years, eight months and six days of the bloodiest conflict in history. Grand Admiral Karl Doenitz surrendered unconditionally to the Allies in a little red schoolhouse at Reims, France. At 8:41 P. M. Sunday, New York time, Col. Gen. Gustav Jodl signed for the enemy and Lieut. Gen. Walter Bedell Smith, General Eisenhower's Chief of Staff, for the Allies. In the absence of any official announcement there was some confusion as to the cessation with the surrender. Fighting had been going on in Czechoslovakia and nothing had been heard from German pockets along the French coast. [1:7-8.]

President Truman planned a broadcast from the White House at 9 o'clock this morning. Wash-

expected to make a simultaneous announcement in Moscow. King George will talk over the radio six hours later. [2:8.] London will celebrate V-E Day today, but, unable to restrain its joy, staged many impromptu celebrations yesterday. [2:7.]

Most New Yorkers took the news calmly and thankfully, sobered by realization that the war in the Pacific was far from over. There were, however, noisy outbursts in such centers as Times Square and Wall Street. Scrap paper showers fluttered from roofs and windows. [1:4-5.]

German Foreign Minister Lutz Schwerin von Krosigk broke the news to his people. The future will be difficult, he warned, and then added: "We must make right the basis of our nation. In our nation justice shall be the

skepticism by the Allies. [2:1.] Perhaps one reason for this was the announcement from Moscow that 4,000,000 men, women and children had been done to death by gas, shooting, famine, poisoning and torture in the German extermination camp at Oswiecim, Poland. [12:8.]

The actual situation in Czechoslovakia was obscure. Late last night a Patriot broadcast said the Germans were negotiating with the Czechoslovak National Council details of surrender in Prague and Bohemia. Fighting had continued throughout yesterday and German planes had bombed public buildings and hospitals. [1:3; map P. 11.]

The United States Third Army continued its general advance into Czechoslovakia and the Fifth and Seventh Armies joined again

Germans were captured. [11:8.]

Japan accepted the surrender of her Axis partner with a statement that she never had expected of German aid and would go on to victory without the Reich. [12:1.]

Infantry and marines on Okinawa scored another general advance after naval bombardment had pulverized Japanese strong points. Pacific Fleet planes sank or damaged thirteen more ships of Korea and Japan. [1:1; map, P. 12.] B-29's maintained their assault on Kyushu airfields. Two of the big planes were shot down. [14:3-4.]

On Tarakan Allied troops were within a mile and a half of the eastern shore. Americans gained on Mindanao and Luzon in the Philippines. [12:3-4.]

Foreign Commissar Molotoff

Concentration camp prisoners hail the arrival of their Allied liberators.

The Holocaust

Early in April 1945, as a company of British soldiers advanced through Germany toward Berlin, they came upon a barbed-wire-enclosed camp. What they saw when they entered the camp sickened them. In trenchlike open graves, piles of naked bodies were stacked like firewood. The soldiers couldn't believe their eyes.

The British troops had entered Belsen

Freed prisoners are marched away from Buchenwald to receive treatment at an American hospital.

These men were prisoners at Dachau in southeast Germany, one of the most infamous concentration camps.

(or Bergen-Belsen), a Nazi concentration camp, about fifty miles south of Hamburg, one of a number built for the imprisonment and mass execution of political prisoners. Most concentration camp victims were European Jews.

The end of World War II and the occupation of Europe by Allied forces revealed the terrible truth that Adolf Hitler had planned to wipe out the entire Jewish population. By the end of the war, the Nazis had killed approximately six million Jewish men, women, and children, a figure that represented about two thirds of the Jewish population in Europe. The word *holocaust*, meaning total destruction of life, is used to describe this horrifying period.

The persecution of Jews under Hitler began soon after the Nazi leader came to power in 1933. Laws were passed that

General Eisenhower (center) tours a Nazi death camp.

deprived Jews of their rights and possessions.

After Hitler invaded the Soviet Union in 1941, the campaign of mass murder began. Jews by the millions were sent to Belsen, Dachau, Buchenwald, Auschwitz, and other camps. Some of the camps had factories in which prisoners were often worked to death. Enormous numbers of men, women, children, and even infants were put to death in gas chambers.

Auschwitz (now Oświęcim), in Poland, was the worst of the concentration camps. Auschwitz was a killing center. More than two and a half million Jews were gassed to death at Auschwitz. Another half a million Jews died of starvation.

As Allied forces moved across the face of Europe, the killing ebbed. The Holocaust ended with the Allied victory in Europe.

Carrier planes above the Saipan beaches during the invasion.

Winning in the Pacific

Once victory had been achieved in Europe, the Allies could focus their energies on defeating Japan. Troops, supplies, ships, and aircraft were quickly shifted from European battle zones to the Pacific.

The strategy was to launch a two-pronged assault. One thrust would begin in the Solomon Islands and New Guinea and surge north and east. The other, originating in the central Pacific, was to involve an island-by-island campaign. As one island group was captured, it would serve as a jumping-off point for the next.

Troops and supplies flooded across the Pacific from west coast ports of the United States. At first, foolish mistakes costing millions of dollars were made. Sugar, for

The first wave of marines hits the beach at Saipan in the Mariana Islands.

Japanese defenders at Saipan hole up in concrete shelters like this one.

instance, was shipped in paper bags, which rotted overnight in tropic rainstorms. Bulldozers then created great islands of sugar in the swamps and piled arriving war material on top of them.

Late in 1943, U.S. Marines had wrested Tarawa and Makin in the Gilbert Islands from the Japanese, although there had been stiff opposition. Early in 1944, U.S. troops captured Kwajalein in the Marshall Islands.

The Mariana Islands were the next target. U.S. Marines, supported by heavy shelling from the Navy ships, landed on the island of Saipan on June 15, 1944. More than 8,000 Marines were put ashore in 20 minutes. The Japanese, who controlled the heights above the beaches, attacked fiercely.

Then an even more serious threat developed. The Japanese fleet steamed into the area. American carriers and battleships were waiting for them. In what has become known in the U.S. Navy as "The Great Marianas Turkey Shoot," American carrier pilots shot down 395 Japanese planes. Japanese losses also included two aircraft carriers.

The destruction of close to four hundred aircraft was a serious blow for the Japa-

Attached to a Marine artillery regiment in the South Pacific, these two Navajo Indians relay orders in their native tongue to prevent the Japanese from intercepting the messages.

Battle-weary marines (right) leave the front lines of Saipan as reserves move up to replace them.

nese. Worse still was the loss of so many pilots. They could not be replaced.

Once the naval battle was won, Allied land forces were assured of success. By mid-July, Saipan was in U.S. hands. Guam and Tinian, two other important islands in the Marianas group, were cleared of Japanese by August.

The Mariana Islands were important because they are about 1,600 miles from Japan, which was within the operating range of the new Boeing B-29 Superfortresses.

Designed for precision bombing from high altitudes, B-29s had been operating from airfields in China, which had been built by some half a million Chinese laborers working with shovels, hoes, and other hand tools. Keeping these bases supplied was a tremendous problem. Fuel, bombs, and everything else had to be ferried from India across the Himalayan Mountains.

Once the Mariana Islands were in American hands, B-29 bases were built immediately. By the fall of 1944, the first raids against Japan were taking place.

Philippine guerillas, some who do not even have shoes, line up before boarding a landing craft for an attack on Japanese positions.

Return to the Philippines

"What do we do next?" That was the question American military leaders sought to answer once the Mariana Islands had been brought under Allied control.

Some strategists wanted to bypass the Philippine Islands and invade Iwo Jima or Okinawa, islands much closer to Japan than the Philippines. Others wanted to launch an attack on Kyushu, the southernmost island in the Japanese chain.

But General Douglas MacArthur, who had promised the Filipinos that he would return, argued that the Allies were duty bound to drive the Japanese out of the

On a Philippine beach, American soldiers unload supplies from a pair of Landing Ship-Tanks.

Philippines before they did anything else. MacArthur won out. On October 20, 1944, U.S. Army troops stormed ashore on two beaches on the central Philippine island of Leyte. MacArthur himself waded ashore about five hours after the first landings.

When the Japanese Navy attempted to destroy the Allied ships supporting the Leyte landings, the result was the Battle of Leyte Gulf, the biggest naval engagement in history and a stunning victory for the Allies. Japan lost four carriers, three

battleships, nine cruisers, and eight destroyers. The Imperial Japanese Navy had been destroyed as a fighting force. The cost to the American Navy was one light carrier, two escort carriers, and three smaller ships.

Allied naval forces were able to score their historic victory despite a new and desperate Japanese tactic — kamikazes, pilots on suicide missions. The word *kamikaze* means "divine wind." It was first used to describe a typhoon that had de-

The hangar deck of the <u>Sangamon</u> is in ruins after the kamikaze attack.

A Japanese kamikaze plane makes a suicide dive near the escort carrier <u>Sangamon</u>.

stroyed an enemy fleet sent to attack Japan in 1281.

Young Japanese pilots locked them-selves in the cockpits of planes that were loaded with explosives and carried only enough fuel to get them where they were

General Douglas MacArthur (left), with Lieutenant General Richard Sutherland at his side, wades through the surf as he returns to the Philippines at the invasion of Leyte Island in October 1944.

Wrecked buildings in Manila, capital of the Philippines, following months of bombing by Japanese planes.

going but not back. Once over their target, they plunged straight down into it. Pilots volunteered for kamikaze missions because they believed it an honor to die for their emperor.

The Battle of Leyte Gulf lasted only a few days but the struggle to gain control of Leyte and the other Philippine Islands ground on and on. After subduing the Japanese forces on Leyte, many troops landed on the island of Luzon at a point about 110 miles north of Manila, the capital of the Philippines. By the end of February 1945, Manila was in Allied hands. But the Japanese continued to resist in the Philippines until the war's end.

The B-29 Superfortress, the biggest bombing plane of World War II, demolished much of Japan, city by city.

Devastation in Tokyo following the B-29 raids.

Attacking Japan by Air and Sea

The four-engine B-29 Superfortress, the biggest bomber of World War II, did more than any other weapon to bring about Japan's defeat. It could carry a bombload of almost eight tons, fly at speeds of up to 350 miles an hour at altitudes of over 35,000 feet, and, most important, with its range of 3,500 miles, make the trip to Tokyo and return to bases in the Mariana Islands.

In March 1945, huge fleets of B-29s from the Marianas began nighttime low-level bombing, dropping incendiary bombs. The results were horrifying. In the first raid, B-29s gutted nearly 16 square miles in the center of Tokyo. More than a quarter of a million buildings were destroyed; almost 9,000 people died. The cities of Osaka, Kobe, and Nagoya were also demolished. The total dead for these raids was 200,000.

While Japanese cities were being re-duced to ashes from the air, American submarines preyed upon the Japanese merchant fleet. As a result, the Japanese were soon starved not only for petroleum, rubber, and various war materials, but also for food and other necessities. Japan was being strangled.

While the B-29s operating from the Mariana Islands had dealt heavy punishment to the Japanese, the aircraft faced many difficulties. Fighter planes to protect the bombers could not fly the entire distance from the Marianas to Japan and back. The B-29s had to make the trip unescorted. The solution to this problem was to move in closer, to capture islands nearer to Japan that could be used for fighter bases.

Iwo Jima and Okinawa, each several hundred miles nearer to Japan than the Marianas, were two of the islands chosen. Military strategists made plans to invade one, then the other.

A marine, his rifle close at hand, reads a stack of mail in an Iwo Jima foxhole.

Carrying their weapons on their shoulders, machine gunners advance in single file on Iwo Jima.

Iwo Jima and Okinawa

I wo Jima is a tiny volcanic island in the Bonin chain, about 750 miles south of Tokyo. George Bush, a 22-year-old Navy lieutenant and carrier pilot at the time, took part in the campaign to gain control of the island.

Several months before the first landings, Bush and other members of his squadron were assigned to bomb a communications center on Chichi Jima, another of the Bonins. During the attack, Bush's TBF Avenger was struck by antiaircraft fire and the future President was forced to bail out. His two crew members did not survive the mission. Bush, who served as a Navy pilot

As a twenty-two-year-old Navy lieutenant and carrier pilot, George Bush takes part in the struggle to gain control of Okinawa. He would later become the forty-first president of the United States.

Victorious American soldiers raise the flag at Iwo Jima. This would become a classic photograph, and the basis for a dramatic war memorial in Washington, D.C.

for more than three years, described the incident as "the worst hours I spent during the war."

U.S. Marines stormed ashore on Iwo Jima in mid-February 1945. The Japanese defenders, hidden in a network of underground caves they had built, resisted stubbornly. The Marines fought their way forward, yard by yard. More than 6,000 Marines died in the six weeks of fighting.

Okinawa, about 350 miles south of Kyushu, the most southern of the Japanese home islands, was next. Again the Japanese fought fanatically. The fleet supporting the invasion had to endure wave after wave of kamikaze attacks. Many hundreds

of suicide planes were involved. Thirty-four naval vessels were sunk and four aircraft carriers damaged.

Okinawa was the last major battle of World War II. It was also one of the costliest. There were 47,000 American casualties, including 12,500 killed.

It seemed that the closer the Allies got to the home islands of Japan, the more desperately the Japanese fought. The U.S. Army believed to defeat Japan it was going to be necessary to invade their home islands and overrun the entire country. They planned to use Okinawa as a springboard for the invasion, which was given the code name "Operation Olympic."

Colonel Paul W. Tibbets, Jr., pilot of the Enola Gay, the plane that dropped the atomic bomb on Hiroshima, seen in his cockpit before takeoff on August 6, 1945.

The Atomic Bomb

In the early morning hours of August 6, 1945, a silvery B-29 Superfortress named the *Enola Gay* eased into the air from Tinian Island in the Marianas. It carried the first atomic bomb to be used in warfare. The plane's target was the Japanese city of Hiroshima.

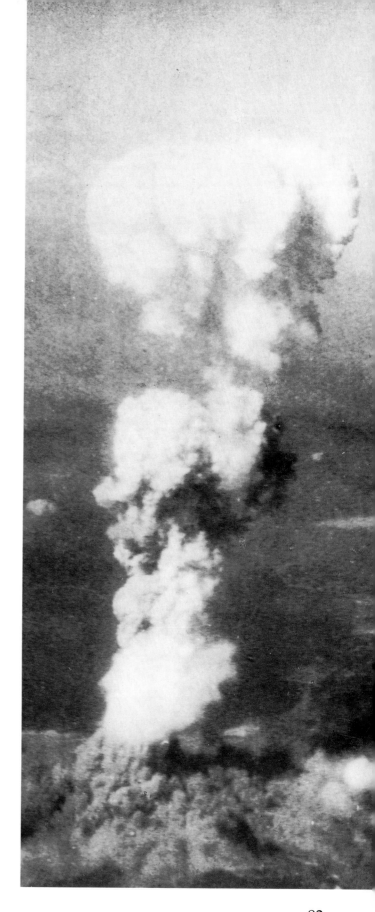

A towering column of smoke rises in the sky over the city of Hiroshima following the dropping of the first atomic bomb.

At 8:15 A.M., Hiroshima time, the bomb was dropped. There was a blinding flash of light. At the same time, people, houses, cars, and buildings vanished into dust. The white-hot dust rose in a great white cloud over the ruins of the city. Fires broke out everywhere. About 80,000 people died.

President Harry S Truman made the decision to drop the atomic bomb. When Truman had become President a few months earlier, he didn't know the atomic bomb existed. One of the first things he was told after President Roosevelt's death was that the United States had in its possession a new type of weapon whose enormous power was created by splitting the atom. American and British scientists had been working on the problem of nuclear fission since 1939.

The New York Times.

Copyright, 1945, by The New York Times Company.

LATE CITY EDITION
Partly cloudy, less humid today.
Cloudy and warm tomorrow.
Temperature Yesterday—Max., 72; Min., 66
Sunrise today, 5:39 A. M.; Sunset, 8:06 P. M.

VOL. XCIV..No. 31,972.

Entered as Second-Class Matter,
Postoffice, New York, N. Y.

NEW YORK, TUESDAY, AUGUST 7, 1945.

THREE CENTS IN NEW YORK CITY

FIRST ATOMIC BOMB DROPPED ON JAPAN; MISSILE IS EQUAL TO 20,000 TONS OF TNT; TRUMAN WARNS FOE OF A 'RAIN OF RUIN'

HIRAM W. JOHNSON, REPUBLICAN DEAN IN THE SENATE, DIES

Isolationist Helped Prevent U. S. Entry Into League—Opposed World Charter

CALIFORNIA EX-GOVERNOR

Ran for Vice President With Theodore Roosevelt in '12 —In Washington Since '17

Special to The New York Times.

WASHINGTON, Aug. 6—Senator Hiram Warren Johnson of California, lifelong isolationist who helped prevent this country's entry into the League of Nations and fought all "foreign entanglements" through a second World War, died in his sleep this morning at Bethesda Naval Hospital, nine days after, ill but consistent, he had paired his vote against ratification of the United Nations Charter. Death was caused by a thrombosis of a cerebral artery. Mrs. Johnson was with him when the end came.

When word reached the Capitol of the passing of the oldest member of the Senate in point of service, save Senator Kenneth McKellar, the President pro tempore, the mourning was deep. With great personal affection colleagues paid humble tribute to his integrity of character, his liberalism and his steadfastness to his ideals and convictions. They joined in declaring that the country had lost a great statesman.

Senator Johnson, who was serving the fourth year of his fifth term in the Senate, would have been 79 years old on Sept. 2. Although his health had been failing during the last two years and though the thundering voice which had conveyed his eloquence through innumerable stirring debates had become little more than a whisper, friends believed he planned to seek a sixth term in 1947.

He went to the hospital July 18. Five days before that he had cast the lone vote in the Foreign Relations Committee, of which he was the ranking minority member, against reporting the new World Charter to the Senate without change. He did not participate in the floor debate on this document, which won Senate approval by a vote of 82–2. However, he clashed spiritedly with colleagues while the hearings were in progress.

Funeral arrangements awaited the arrival of the Senator's son, Lieut. Col. Hiram W. Johnson Jr., who was flying here from California.

Capper Becomes the Dean

The death of Senator Johnson made Senator Arthur Capper of Kansas, who last month marked his eighty-first birthday, the Republican dean of the Senate. It also elevated him to the ranking minority membership on the Foreign Relations Committee, of which Senator Johnson had been so conspicuously identified through the many years of his unshaken position on foreign policy. Mr. Capper, too, with Senators McKellar, Carter Glass of Virginia, David I. Walsh of Massachusetts and Peter G. Gerry, was in the League fight of 1919 and 1920. He supported it with reservations.

The career of Senator Johnson, from his entrance into the Senate from the Governorship of California in March of 1917, was one distinctly lacking in compromise or reservation. In 1912 he had bolted his party with Theodore Roosevelt and had become his running mate on the Bull Moose ticket. In 1932 he again bolted to support Franklin D. Roosevelt for the Presidency but broke bitterly with the President when he ran for his third term.

In 1912 Mr. Johnson joined with Senators Lodge, Borah, Reed,

Continued on Page 23, Column 4

Jet Plane Explosion Kills Major Bong, Top U. S. Ace

Flier Who Downed 40 Japanese Craft, Sent Home to Be 'Safe,' Was Flying New 'Shooting Star' as a Test Pilot

By The United Press.

BURBANK, Calif., Aug. 6—Maj. Richard Bong, America's greatest air ace, died today in the flaming wreckage of a jet propelled fighter plane which crashed while he was testing it.

Only 24 years old, he wore twenty-six decorations including the nation's highest award, the Congressional Medal of Honor. He had survived countless air battles and shot down forty Japanese planes without a scratch.

The knowledge he gained in those battles was too valuable to risk, so he was brought home to "safe" duty. He was on that "safe" duty today when his P-80, the Shooting Star, hurtled over a clump of trees and burst like a bomb in a field.

Witnesses did not agree on the cause of the crash. One Army flier said that Major Bong overshot the Lockheed airport. Another witness, John McKinney of North Hollywood reported that he saw something fall out of the plane's tail.

"The plane started to wobble up and down, then went into a left bank and hit the ground," he stated. "It exploded and burned and scattered wreckage over about a block square."

Major Bong was trying to get out of the ship when it crashed. He had released the escape hatch and was partly clear. He had pulled the ripcord to his parachute, and the silken folds lay about the body as the flames swept over it.

With a roaring sigh, the plane, like a giant blowtorch, shot over the airport just before 3 P. M. and then lurched over the trees and nosed down into the field, a mile away.

Smoke and flame surged up and crowds rushed from the airport. By the time anyone could reach the scene the ship had been almost consumed.

The crash scene was near the intersection of Cahuenga and Oxnard Boulevards and barely out-

Continued on page 15, Column 2

KYUSHU CITY RAZED

Kenney's Planes Blast Tarumizu in Record Blow From Okinawa

ROCKET SITE IS SEEN

125 B-29's Hit Japan's Toyokawa Naval Arsenal in Demolition Strike

By FRANK L. KLUCKHOHN

MANILA, Tuesday, Aug. 7—More than 400 fighters and bombers, appearing at chimney-top level for two hours Sunday over Tarumizu in southern Kyushu in the largest single attack launched by Gen. George C. Kenney's Far East Air Forces to date, wrecked that city's munitions factories and aircraft and munitions storage depots and waterfront installations.

Rockets and demolition bombs were poured by waves of B-26 Invaders, B-25 Mitchells and Mustangs and Thunderbolts of the Fifth and Seventh Air Forces from Okinawa, supported by a few B-24 Liberators carrying big bombs.

Tarumizu, about 350 miles from Okinawa, appeared to be a site at which the Japanese might be preparing a rocket campaign against the American base, said a United Press dispatch. FEAF pilots reported seeing in the area, which has extensive cave construction, what seemed to be Japanese robot planes and also a huge catapult-like machine, extending over the water, that might be a rocket launcher.

[About 125 B-29's hit the Toyokawa naval arsenal of Japan in a demolition bombing Tuesday noon, Strategic Air Forces headquarters at Guam reported.]

The planes over Tarumizu met scant resistance, as our fliers took their time to assure the highest

Continued on Page 11, Column 2

REPORT BY BRITAIN

'By God's Mercy' We Beat Nazis to Bomb, Churchill Says

ROOSEVELT AID CITED

Raiders Wrecked Norse Laboratory in Race for Key to Victory

The text of Mr. Churchill's statement is on page 4.

By CLIFTON DANIEL

LONDON, Aug. 6—The hitherto secret details of the grisly race between Germany and the Allies to find a weapon so destructive that it would insure absolute victory—a race not only between scientists but also between under-cover agents—were recounted in London tonight after it had been disclosed that the first atomic bomb had been dropped on Japan.

"By God's mercy British and American science outpaced all German efforts," said a statement by former Prime Minister Churchill written before he left office and issued from 10 Downing Street by his successor, Clement R. Attlee.

"The possession of these powers by the Germans at any time might have altered the result of the war," Mr. Churchill said, "and profound anxiety was felt by those who were informed."

The British Isles, which endured the terrors of flying bombs and rockets, did hear repeated warnings that Adolf Hitler's V-3 weapon was to be an atomic bomb, but they never knew until tonight how close they came to being the first victims of its destructive power. Much less did they suspect what

Continued on Page 9, Column 1

Steel Tower 'Vaporized' In Trial of Mighty Bomb

Scientists Awe-Struck as Blinding Flash Lighted New Mexico Desert and Great Cloud Bore 40,000 Feet Into Sky

By LEWIS WOOD

Special to The New York Times.

WASHINGTON, Aug. 6—A blinding flash many times as brilliant as the midday sun and a massive, multi-colored cloud boiling up 40,000 feet into the air accompanied the first test firing of an atomic bomb on July 16, three weeks ago today. Set in the desert wastelands of New Mexico, the experiment was seen against a wild background where rain poured in torrents, and lightning pierced the sky up to the zero hour of the explosion at 5:30 A. M.

A steel tower from which the atomic weapon hung was vaporized. In its place was only a huge, sloping crater. At the moment of the explosion a mountain range three miles distant stood out in gigantic in brilliant light.

"Then," said the War Department in a description, "came a tremendous, sustained roar and a heavy pressure wave which knocked down two men outside the control tower (10,000 yards, or more than five miles, away.)"

Before the detonation scientists waited in tense expectancy. Minutes lengthened seemingly to hours. Lying face downward, with their feet toward the steel tower, the watchers waited, nearly breathless. They were "reaching into the unknown" and did not know what would happen.

On the instant that all war over these men leaped to their feet. The terrible tension ended, they shook hands, embraced each other and shouted in glee. Behind their triumph was sober consciousness of possessing the means to "insure the speedy conclusion of the war and save thousands of American lives."

The scene of the great drama was the Alamogordo Air Base, 120 miles southeast of Albuquerque. Here the scientists strove to unlock the secret upon which $2,000,000,000 had been spent. Graphic word pictures of the

Continued on Page 5, Column 1

NEW AGE USHERED

Day of Atomic Energy Hailed by President, Revealing Weapon

HIROSHIMA IS TARGET

'Impenetrable' Cloud of Dust Hides City After Single Bomb Strikes

Truman, Stimson statements on atomic bomb, Page 4.

By SIDNEY SHALETT

Special to The New York Times.

WASHINGTON, Aug. 6—The White House and War Department announced today that an atomic bomb, possessing more power than 20,000 tons of TNT, a destructive force equal to the load of 2,000 B-29's and more than 2,000 times the blast power of what previously was the world's most devastating bomb, had been dropped on Japan.

The announcement, first given to the world in utmost solemnity by President Truman, made it plain that one of the scientific landmarks of the century had been passed, and that its "rays of destruction" were a tremendous force for the advancement of civilization as well as for destruction, was at hand.

At 10:45 o'clock this morning, a statement by the President was issued at the White House that sixteen hours earlier—an American plane had dropped the single atomic bomb on the Japanese city of Hiroshima, an important army center.

Japanese Solemnly Warned

What happened at Hiroshima is not yet known. The War Department said it "as yet was unable to make an accurate report" because "an impenetrable cloud of dust and smoke" masked the target area from reconnaissance planes. The Secretary of War will release the story "as soon as accurate details of the results of the bombing become available."

But in a statement vividly describing the results of the first test of the atomic bomb in New Mexico, the War Department told how an immense steel tower had been "vaporized" by the tremendous explosion, how a 40,000-foot cloud rushed into the sky, and two observers were knocked down at a point 10,000 yards away. And President Truman solemnly warned:

"It was to spare the Japanese people from utter destruction that the ultimatum of July 26 was issued at Potsdam. Their leaders promptly rejected that ultimatum. If they do not now accept our terms, they may expect a rain of ruin from the air the like of which has never been seen on this earth."

Most Closely Guarded Secret

The President referred to the joint statement issued by the heads of the American, British and Chinese Governments, in which terms of surrender were outlined that rejection would mean complete destruction of Japan's power to make war.

[The atomic bomb weighs about 400 pounds and is capable of utterly destroying a town, a representative of the British Ministry of Aircraft Production said in London, the United Press reported.]

What is this terrible new weapon, which the War Department also calls the "Cosmic Bomb"? It is the harnessing of the energy of the atom, which is the basic power of the universe. As President Truman said, "The force from which the sun draws its power has been loosed against those who brought war to the Far East."

"Atomic fission"—in other

Continued on Page 2, Column 3

MORRIS IS ACCUSED OF 'TAKING A WALK'

Fusion Official 'Sad to Part Company'—McGoldrick Sees Only Tammany Aided

The No Deal ticket, headed by Council President Newbold Morris, "can only serve the interests of Tammany Hall," Controller Joseph D. McGoldrick, candidate for re-election on the Republican-Liberal-Fusion party slate, declared yesterday in a frank attack on the third-party ticket injected over the week-end into the city Mayoralty campaign.

Swaying block-by-block street fighting is raging in the strategic coastal highway town, 121 miles southwest of Canton, a communiqué said.

By breaking into Yeungkong Chinese forces won control of a fifty-mile coastal stretch leading west to Tinpak, which lies well open to a virtually unopposed landing should American forces choose it for a staging point for supplies to the armies of South China.

A short while later Gabriel A. Wechsler, general secretary of the City Fusion party, which supported Mayor La Guardia and Mr. Morris in previous city campaigns, accused Mr. Morris of "taking a walk away from the good government forces."

To both charges Mr. Morris declared he would stand on his statement of Sunday that he was not interested in "just taking votes" away from Judge Jonah J. Goldstein. Republican-Liberal-Fusion candidate for Mayor, or from William O'Dwyer, his Democratic-American Labor party opponent.

"I have no comment," he said, "since I stand on my statement of Sunday. We are waging an affirmative campaign."

Informed that Hyman Blumberg,

Continued on Page 19, Column 6

CHINESE WIN MORE OF 'INVASION COAST'

Smash Into Port 121 Miles Southwest of Canton—Big Area Open for Landing

By The Associated Press.

CHUNGKING, China, Aug. 6—Chinese troops have broken into the South China port of Yeungkong and cleared a fifty-mile stretch of the Chinese "invasion coast" west of Hong Kong, Generalissimo Chiang Kai-shek's headquarters said today.

West of Luchow Peninsula another 145-mile coastal stretch extending to the Indo-China frontier is under Chinese control and observers believe the Chinese soon may launch a concerted drive from the west and east that would seal off the Japanese on the Luchow

Continued on Page 2, Column 2

War News Summarized

TUESDAY, AUGUST 7, 1945

One bomb hit Japan on Sunday night, but it struck with the force of 20,000 tons of TNT. Where it landed had been the city of Hiroshima; what is there now has not yet been learned.

The attack, dramatically announced by President Truman sixteen hours after the missile had struck, was with an atomic bomb, a "harnessing of the basic power of the universe," he said. "The force from which the sun draws its power has been loosed against those who brought war to the Far East. And the end is not yet."

Details of the missile are closely guarded, but the 125,000 workers who saw materials pour into their factories never saw anything go out. The bomb is the result of pooling British-American scientific knowledge begun in 1940. "We have spent two billion dollars on the greatest scientific gamble in history —and won," Mr. Truman said.

"We are now prepared to obliterate more rapidly and completely every productive enterprise the Japanese have above ground in any city. It was to spare the Japanese public from utter destruction that the ultimatum of July 26 was issued at Potsdam. If they do not accept our terms they may expect a rain of ruin from the air."

Secretary of War Stimson detailed the story of research and production and forecast improvements to increase the effectiveness of the "atomic bomb" several times. [1:4.]

Hiroshima was a major military target, a city of 318,000 persons thickly settled around quartermaster's depot, an em-

All production was in the United States at two plants at Oak Ridge, near Knoxville, Tenn., and one at Richland, Wash. A scientific laboratory was maintained in Santa Fe, N. M. [1:4.]

Former Prime Minister Churchill told of Britain's part, including costly attacks on German "heavy water" plants and the race to outstrip the Nazis. He praised American scientific achievement and gave full credit to President Roosevelt and his advisers. [1:3.]

Tokyo made no mention of what had happened to Hiroshima but rail service in that area was canceled. [1:7.]

Okinawa sent out 400 planes that left Tarumizu, on Kyushu's Kagoshima Bay, in flaming wreckage. About 125 "Superforts" bombed Toyokawa naval arsenal by daylight. [1:4; map p. 11.]

Chinese troops have broken into the port of Yeungkong and have cleared a large stretch of the south China coast west of Hong Kong and east of the Luichow Peninsula. [1:3; map P. 2.]

Moscow, moving to implement diplomatic relations with Finland and Rumania. [11:4.]

The Germans received an opportunity to develop democratic talents when the United States and Great Britain authorized local trade unions and political parties in their zones of occupation. [12:2.]

France is expected to ratify the United Nations Charter and then the Bretton Woods monetary plan in the near future. [13:6.] Marshal Pétain is accused of having asked Hitler for help in regaining France's colonies. [13:1.]

ATOM BOMBS MADE IN 3 HIDDEN 'CITIES'

Secrecy on Weapon So Great That Not Even Workers Knew of Their Product

By JAY WALZ

WASHINGTON, Aug. 6—The War Department revealed today how three "hidden cities" with a terrific damage in their making, were used in producing the materials and the uranium that goes into a new atomic bomb. The secrecy was so great that of the 100,000 atomic bomb project, how they did their work without knowing what it was all about, and how they kept the biggest secret of the war.

One of these, Oak Ridge, situated where only oak and pine trees had dotted small farms before, is today the fifth largest city in Tennessee. The population of 75,000 persons has thirteen supermarkets, nine drug stores and seven theatres.

A second town of 7,000 was built for reasons of isolation and recurity on a New Mexico mesa. The third, named Richland Village, houses 17,000 men, women and children on remote banks of the Columbia River in the State of Washington.

None of the people, who came to these developments from homes all the way from Maine to California, had the slightest idea of what they were making in the gigantic Gov-

Continued on Page 3, Column 2

TRAINS CANCELED IN STRICKEN AREA

Traffic Around Hiroshima Is Disrupted—Japanese Still Sift Havoc by Split Atoms

By The United Press.

WASHINGTON, Aug. 6—The Osaka radio, without referring to the atomic bomb dropped on Hiroshima, hinted tonight at the terrific damage it must have caused by announcing that train service in the Hiroshima and other areas had been canceled.

First mention of the bomb came in a Japanese Domei agency dispatch announcing that President Truman and Prime Minister Attlee had disclosed that the new missile had been dropped on Hiroshima.

The Office of War Information began telling the Japanese today what hit them. OWI branch transmitters in San Francisco, Hawaii and Saipan beamed President Truman's statement on the atomic bomb to Japan.

Edward Barrett, director of the OWI's overseas branch, said that President's announcement and related information on the atomic bomb will dominate the OWI's normal Japanese transmissions for the next several days.

LONDON, Tuesday, Aug. 7 (UP) —The Japanese Domei news agency, in a dispatch recorded by the British radio, said today that

Cont'nued on Page 7, Column 1

Turks Talk War if Russia Presses; Prefer Vain Battle to Surrender

By SAM POPE BREWER

By Wireless to The New York Times.

ANKARA, Turkey, Aug. 6—Russo-Turkish relations weigh heavy on Turkish minds these days. All leading editions comment today on various aspects of the Russian claims against Turkey.

The Potsdam conference leaves the situation virtually unchanged so far as the Turks can see, but they seem to agree that they would go to war, however hopeless such a war might be, rather than yield before the threat of force. Suggestions from London and Washington that the Russians have been asked to moderate their demands give little reassurance here.

The Potsdam communiqué created more confusion than confidence and the Turks are still trying to decide whether the fact that the conference did not deal with certain questions means that it was a failure.

Many point out that all the really thorny questions still are unsettled. The Turks probably do not see a relative importance among world problems of Russian demands on Turkey, but point out that the important question of principle is involved. The general and apparently official argument is that the status of the Straits cannot be modified by a bilateral agreement but must be discussed at a conference of the signatories of the Montreux Convention, with America replacing Japan. The signatories were Great Britain, France, Russia, Japan, Turkey, Greece, Rumania, Yugoslavia and Bulgaria.

The grounds for the Russian claims to Kars and Ardahan are not clear, but throughout the Near and Mideast in recent months

Continued on Page 18, Column 1

Reich Exile Emerges as Heroine In Denial to Nazis of Atom's Secret

Special to The New York Times.

WASHINGTON, Aug. —G—How Germany twice narrowly missed the secret of harnessing atomic energy by splitting uranium atoms and releasing the most powerful destructive force on earth was reached today in War Department reports on the atomic bomb.

Development of the bomb after more than ten years of experimentation and research marks the first time that Prof. Albert Einstein's theory of relativity has been put to practical use outside the laboratory; the equation by which he showed the existence of a definite relationship of matter, energy and the velocity of light.

That the new bomb may be far from its maximum devastating power, that the energy we are now able to utilize in the atomic bombs, at 100 per cent efficiency, constitutes

total energy present in the material. But even one-hundredth of 1 per cent is still the most destructive force so far on this earth."

The principal character in the dramatic story of the long search for a method of releasing atomic energy is Dr. Lise Meitner, a woman physicist whom the Nazis expelled from Germany as a "non-Aryan." With her associates, Dr. Otto Hahn and Dr. F. Strassmann, she was working in the Kaiser Wilhelm Institute in Berlin, bombarding uranium atoms with neutrons and then submitting the uranium to chemical analysis.

As the War Department tells the story:

To their amazement, they found the element barium in the debris of the smashed uranium atoms.

Continued on Page 7, Column 1

The nuclear blast destroyed sixty percent of Hiroshima within two minutes.

A test bomb was exploded at Los Alamos, New Mexico, on July 16, 1945. Ten days later at the Potsdam Conference in the ruins of Berlin, Truman and other Allied leaders issued an ultimatum to Japan, demanding unconditional surrender. The Japanese government did not respond in a positive way. Truman then ordered the atomic bomb to be dropped.

Truman knew his decision was a fateful one that future generations would debate whether it was the right decision. But the President felt millions of Japanese and Americans would die if the Allies had to invade Japan. Truman believed he had no other choice.

Japanese officials arrive aboard the U.S.S. Missouri in Tokyo Bay to sign the surrender agreement.

Victory

Three days after the bombing of Hiroshima, a second atomic bomb was dropped. This time the city of Nagasaki was the target. Another 40,000 people vanished in a sudden burst of flame and smoke. Almost at the same time, the Soviet Union launched a massive attack on Japanese forces in Manchuria.

That was enough for the Japanese. They decided to accept the Allies' surrender terms, provided their emperor could remain on the throne.

Japan's message of surrender reached President Truman late in the afternoon of August 14, 1945. When, at 7 P.M. the President announced the news to the wait-

"All the News
That's Fit to Print"

The New York Times.

NEWS INDEX, PAGE 23, THIS SECTION

Copyright, 1945, by The New York Times Company.

LATE CITY EDITION
Clearing early today; cooler.
Clear and cool tomorrow.
Temperature Yesterday—Max., 88; Min., 72
Seattle today, 6:33 A. M.; Sunset, 7:38 P. M.

Section
1

VOL. XCIV. No. 31,998.
Entered as Second-Class Matter,
Postoffice, New York, N. Y.

NEW YORK, SUNDAY, SEPTEMBER 2, 1945.

Including Magazine
and Book Review.

TEN CENTS
New York City and Suburban Areas (3c Elsewhere)

JAPAN SURRENDERS TO ALLIES, SIGNS RIGID TERMS ON WARSHIP; TRUMAN SETS TODAY AS V-J DAY

HOLIDAY TRAFFIC NEAR 1941 LEVEL; 'GAS' IS PLENTIFUL

Exodus From City Is Greatest Since Pre-War Days but Congestion Is Avoided

GOOD WEATHER PROMISED

Near-by Resorts Do Capacity Business—3 Persons Die in Queens Accidents

America's millions, deprived since 1941 of the chance to cruise the highways of their nation, hit the road in traditional Labor Day week-end style yesterday.

There was a plentiful supply of gasoline, the sun shone warm out of blue skies, and everyone felt free from war worries. This combined to roll up traffic that continued heavy all day.

New York City's heat-ridden population took to car, train, bus and plane. The exodus to near-by mountain and seashore resorts was the greatest since that of 1941.

The weather formed a perfect lure. Not even the thunder showers predicted by the Weather Bureau for late afternoon took place. Today's prediction is for clearing weather early, followed by cooler, with the highest temperature around 80 degrees, and with fresh to strong northwest winds. A clear and cool Monday is forecast by the bureau. The temperature yesterday reached 88 degrees at 3:30 P. M. with the humidity at 52 per cent. The all-time high for the date was set in 1924 with 92.5 degrees and the low in 1872 with 51.

Many Cars Come Into City

Travel in the city was two-way. Cars streamed out of the city over bridges, on ferries and through tunnels, out-of-towners poured in. The main idea for Labor Day seemed to be change of scenery.

Thousands of automobiles, many of them looking as though they had just been taken off the jacks for the first time in years, formed a continuous procession along the main highways leading up-State, out on Long Island and to the South Jersey shore.

The Port of New York Authority reported that 69,400 automobiles had crossed the George Washington Bridge into New Jersey. Forty-five thousand cars passed through the Holland Tunnel during the sixteen hours preceding 6 o'clock last night. Lincoln Tunnel police said traffic was heavier than usual.

Few serious accidents were reported. "Maybe it's because the cars just don't have the jam," remarked a Westchester County parkway policeman.

Sights along the parkways bore out his contention. Many cars became pathetically silent as their drivers resignedly hauled them over to the side of the road to patch up tires or to fume over engine repairs.

Gasoline Supplies Abundant

Assured of as much gasoline as they wanted, motorists traveled leisurely and did not cause congestion. Filling station pumps received their heaviest workout in years. Station operators estimated that demand for gasoline ranged from 10 to 30 per cent over last week-end, but they reported there was no difficulty in obtaining supplies.

The Cities Service Oil Company said it was having difficulty in meeting orders for premium gasoline, ordinarily accounting for 25 per cent of sales, as the supply was limited, but no company reported shortages of non-premium gasoline. No motorist was forced to stay in town because of lack of fuel.

Trains, buses and airlines were crowded, as they have been all through the war. The airlines re-

Continued on Page 30, Column 2

Times Sq. Takes V-J News Quietly

Times Square throngs, which had greeted Japanese capitulation explosively last month, took the formal signing of terms in much calmer fashion last night. Two hundred policemen, including twenty-five mounted patrolmen, who had been assigned to the area in case of another outburst of feeling, reported that the street crowds took the flashing of the bulletin from Times Tower at 10:04 P. M. with a few cheers and good-natured remarks, and did not attempt to start a celebration.

In numbers the crowd was no larger than an average Saturday night, and of the persons present perhaps half or more were out-of-town visitors here for the Labor Day week-end, the police estimated. Other parts of the city were similarly quiet.

Mayor La Guardia had said earlier that the people "have had their big time and are satisfied." He declined not to hold a celebration in Central Park today as had been planned.

PRESIDENT STRESSES LABOR DAY OF PEACE

But He Warns That After Six Holidays of Hostilities Great New Problems Lie Ahead

Special to THE NEW YORK TIMES.
WASHINGTON, Sept. 1.—President Truman hailed the first Labor Day of peace in six years today and declared a grateful world would always remember the workers of all free nations for their contribution to victory.

Secretary Forrestal and J. A. Krug, chairman of the War Production Board, also lauded the men and women of labor, and Philip Murray, chairman of the Congress of Industrial Organizations, told a radio audience that America's vast war plant must be put to work on peacetime products which would give prosperity unlimited to this country.

Mr. Truman's statement said that six years ago today the workers of the United States, and of the world, awoke to a Labor Day in a world at war, and added:

"We in the United States had two years of grace, but the issue was squarely joined at that hour, as we now know. There was to be no peace until tyranny had been outlawed.

"Today we stand on the threshold of a new world. We must do our part in making the world what it should be, a world in which the bigotries of race and class and creed shall not be permitted to warp the souls of men.

"We enter upon an era of great problems, but to live is to face problems. Our men and women did not falter in the task of saving freedom. They will not falter now in the task of making freedom

Continued on Page 24, Column 3

HAILS ERA OF PEACE

President Calls On U.S. to Stride On Toward a World of Good-Will

SALUTES HEROIC DEAD

Cautions Jubilant Nation Hard Jobs Ahead Need Same Zeal as War

Text of the President's address proclaiming V-J Day, P. 4.

By WILLIAM S. WHITE
Special to THE NEW YORK TIMES.
WASHINGTON, Sept. 1.—President Truman, in remembrance of all who have fallen and in an appeal to all Americans to go forward now in hope and fraternity toward "a new and better world of peace and international good-will," tonight solemnly proclaimed tomorrow to be V-J Day.

The moment that he began to speak was, in the official and historical sense, the first moment of peace this country had known for years ago, when, at a sudden, a harsh and an incredible blow the whole of the Pacific world went into flames.

Into the human calendar of great American holidays, like the Fourth of July and the Eleventh of November, the President thus entered another date, the Second of September, although it does not technically signify the end of the "duration" and will have no basis as a legal end of the war. The termination of hostilities, for purposes of computing military service, for setting the limit on war agencies and for all other like formalities, will be set only by final decision of Congress.

But Mr. Truman's speech was a speech to the heart of a country that had had the skill to make the atomic bomb and could now "use the same skill and energy and determination to overcome all the difficulties ahead," rather than to the keepers of its books of law.

It was notice from the White House, so long awaited, that nearly four years of war, a struggle of sacrificial grandeur such as the United States had never known, had at last come to an end, and that the terrible ledger opened at Pearl Harbor had now been balanced and closed.

The President spoke in this mood, a mood of valedictory and of dedication, as he proclaimed "this . . . victory of more than arms alone . . . this . . . victory of liberty over tyranny." He had just received the signal from battleship Missouri, on which he signed in behalf of the Allies, said mankind hoped a better world would result from the solemn occasion. [1:8; map P. 12.]

President Truman proclaimed today as V-J Day. He urged the nation to observe the day of victory over Japan in a spirit of dedication and as a symbol of "victory of liberty over tyranny." He also asked his countrymen to remember "our departed gallant leader, Franklin D. Roosevelt."

Continued on Page 4, Column 1

BYRNES FORESEES A PEACEFUL JAPAN

Says People Are Expected to Force Development—World Amity Vital, Hull Warns

Special to THE NEW YORK TIMES.
WASHINGTON, Sept. 1.—Secretary of State James F. Byrnes declared tonight that with Japan's surrender we have entered the second phase of our war—"what might be called the spiritual disarmament of that nation, to make them want peace instead of wanting war."

The intention of this Government

Continued on Page 5, Column 1

World News Summarized

SUNDAY, SEPTEMBER 2, 1945

The rulers of Japan, who set the Pacific ablaze nearly four years ago with their surprise attack on Pearl Harbor and hoped to culminate that assault with a peace dictated in the White House, formally signed their unconditional surrender to the Allied powers in Tokyo Bay. Foreign Minister Shigemitsu signed the historic document for his country in the shadow of the sixteen-inch gun muzzles of the battleship Missouri. Gen. MacArthur, who signed in behalf of the Allies, said mankind hoped a better world would result from the solemn occasion. [1:8; map P. 12.]

Japan's decision to surrender was dictated by Emperor Hirohito after he had overruled a strong faction within the Cabinet and the army that wanted to keep on with the war in the [1:8:7.]

JAPANESE FOREIGN MINISTER SIGNING SURRENDER ARTICLES

Mamoru Shigemitsu (right, seated), on behalf of Emperor Hirohito, affixes his signature to document as Gen. Douglas MacArthur (left) and Lieut. Gen. Richard K. Sutherland (center) look on during ceremony aboard the Missouri in Tokyo Bay.

Associated Press Wirephoto (via Navy Radio from U. S. S. Iowa)

Japan's Surrender Ordered Over Militarist Opposition

By FRANK L. KLUCKHOHN
TOKYO, Sept. 1—In the rubble of this once-proud imperial capital the story of how the Japanese Army opposed the surrender and how the Emperor made the final decision to capitulate after having heard the opinions of all his advisers, and how War Minister Korechika Anami committed suicide was unfolded today by one of a handful of those in a position to know without bias what occurred.

It was also learned how the Japanese reacted step by step to war time developments and how propaganda that Japan could win had been continued to the last moment, thus leaving the industrious long

Continued on Page 7, Column 1

U. S. CHIEFS DIVIDED ON ITALY'S COLONIES

State Department Split Over Russia and Influence Zones Is Projected by Issue

By JAMES B. RESTON
WASHINGTON, Sept. 1—A fundamental issue has developed in the Department of State over the future of the Italian colonies, particularly Eritrea, Libya and Italian Somaliland.

The issue is whether these colonies should go back to Italy as part of her sovereign territory, be taken from her and administered by the United States, Britain, France and the Soviet Union under the United Nations Organization or be administered by a neutral international commission and aboard a United States hospital ship. [1:6-7.]

With the Foreign Ministers Council scheduled to meet in London next week to begin consideration of peace terms, it was learned that a serious division of opinion over the disposition of the Italian colonies had developed in the State Department. [1:8.]

Former Secretary of State Stettinius said in London that the development of the atomic bomb emphasized the need for "the speedy creation of the United Nations Organization to keep the peace of the world" and predicted that as soon as the organization began functioning it would appoint a military staff to deal with the use of atomic bombs, as well as all other types of force, in preserving peace. [18:3.]

WAR COMES TO END

Articles of Capitulation Endorsed by Countries in Pacific Conflict

M'ARTHUR SEES PEACE

Emperor Orders Subjects to Obey All Commands Issued by General

The texts of the surrender documents and statements, P. 3.

By The Associated Press.
ABOARD THE U. S. S. MISSOURI in Tokyo Bay, Sunday, Sept. 2—Japan surrendered formally and unconditionally to the Allies today in a twenty-minute ceremony which ended just as the sun burst through low-hanging clouds as a shining symbol to a ravaged world now done with war.

[A United Press dispatch said the leading Japanese delegate signed the articles at 9:03 A. M. Sunday, Tokyo time, and that General MacArthur signed them at 9:07 A. M.]

Twelve signatures, requiring only a few minutes to inscribe on the articles of surrender, ended the bloody Pacific conflict.

On behalf of Emperor Hirohito, Foreign Minister Mamoru Shigemitsu signed for the Government and Gen. Yoshijiro Umezu for the Imperial General Staff.

MacArthur Voices Peace Hope

Gen. Douglas MacArthur then accepted in behalf of the United Nations, declaring:

"It is my earnest hope and indeed the hope of all mankind that from this solemn occasion a better world shall emerge out of the blood and carnage of the past."

One by one the Allied representatives stepped forward and signed the document that blighted Japan's dream of empire built on bloodshed and tyranny.

First was Admiral Chester W. Nimitz for the United States, then the representatives of China, the United Kingdom, the Soviet, Australia, Canada, France, the Netherlands and New Zealand.

The flags of the United States, Britain, the Soviet and China fluttered from the veranda deck of the famed superdreadnaught, polished and scrubbed as never before. More than 100 high-ranking military and naval officers watched.

Pledges Justice and Tolerance

Surrounded by the might of the United States Navy and Army, and under the eyes of the Americans and British commanders they so ruthlessly defeated in the Philippines and Malaya, the Japanese representatives quietly made their marks on paper that ended the bloody Pacific conflict.

The Japanese delegation came aboard at 8:55 A. M., 7:55 P. M. Eastern war time. As scheduled. They reached the Missouri in personnel speed boats flying the American flag.

Foreign Minister Mamoru Shigemitsu led the delegation. His climbed stiffly up the ladder and limped forward on his right leg, which is artificial. His was wounded by a bomb tossed by a Korean terrorist in Shanghai many years ago.

On behalf of Emperor Hirohito, Mr. Shigemitsu signed the surrender document.

TOKYO AIDES WEEP AS GENERAL SIGNS

Imperial Staff Chief Hastily Scrawls His Signature— Shigemitsu Is Anxious

By The Associated Press
ABOARD U. S. S. MISSOURI in Tokyo Bay, Sunday, Sept. 2—The solemn surrender ceremony, on this battleship today, marking the first defeat in Japan's 2,600-year-old semi-legendary history, required only a few minutes as twelve signatures were affixed to the articles.

Continued on Page 9, Column 1

PRESIDENT STRESSES LABOR DAY OF PEACE

Public Gets Big Army Food Stocks; Whipping Cream Is Freed of Bans

Special to THE NEW YORK TIMES.
WASHINGTON, Sept. 1.—The national food situation continued its steady improvement today as the Department of Agriculture, with four orders, increased the supplies of butter, canned salmon and ice cream and signaled the return of whipping cream.

This action was a direct consequence of the sharp reduction of military requirements of these foods. With the discontinuance of butter purchases by the armed forces, the Department explained, it is now possible to revoke the limitations on the sale of heavy cream and the use of butter fat in the production of all frozen desserts. Both these rulings will make

whipping cream and ice cream of a higher butter fat content readily available.

In a simultaneous direction, the agency ordered released for civilian use all butter currently held by creameries and receivers for the armed forces and other Government buyers. Although as much as 20,000,000 pounds of butter may be returned to civilian consumers under this ruling, ration values will not be changed, it was indicated.

"At the time ration point values were established for butter," the Office of Price Administration "recognized the possibility of release

Continued on Page 55, Column 1

Food Dilemma? Read Margaret Roberts on the Woman's Page of the Brooklyn Eagle.—Advt.

Enemy Tortured Dying Americans With Sadist Medical 'Experiments'

By ROBERT TRUMBULL
By Wireless to THE NEW YORK TIMES.
ABOARD THE HOSPITAL SHIP BENEVOLENCE, in Tokyo Bay, Sept. 1 — Seriously ailing American prisoners at Shinagawa, the only hospital serving 8,000 prisoners of war held in the Tokyo area, were guinea pigs for fantastic experiments recalling the sorcery and sadism of the middle ages, Drs. Mack L. Gottlieb and Harold W. Keschner, both of New York, told this correspondent today.

Both doctors are recuperating from Shinagawa on Wednesday by a special Navy evacuation mission headed by Comdr. Harold A. Stassen, former Governor of Min-

belief that the Japanese could defeat an invasion of the homeland, according to well-informed observers in Tokyo. [1:5-6.]

Medical "experiments" recalling medieval sadism were carried out on dying American prisoners of war by young Japanese Army doctors, two American physicians interned with their compatriots said aboard a United States hospital ship. [1:6-7.]

With the Foreign Ministers Council scheduled to meet in London next week to begin consideration of peace terms, it was learned that a serious division of opinion over the disposition of the Italian colonies had developed in the State Department. [1:8.]

The major powers that defeated Germany are soon to start draft-

Continued on Page 15, Column 1

the experiment recalling the sorcery and sadism of the middle ages, Drs. Mack L. Gottlieb and Harold W. Keschner, both of New York, told this correspondent today.

Dr. Gottlieb, who had his home and office at 207 East Forty-fourth Street, was a Naval officer captured at Guam. Dr. Keschner, of 681 West End Avenue, was taken with an Army force in the Philippines. Both are in good physical

Continued on Page 14, Column 1

"ALL THE NEWS THAT'S FIT TO PRINT"

In the first eight months of this year, The Times published 6,092 more columns of news than any other newspaper. With World Peace still to be won, and reconversion a topic of daily import, The New York Times continues to print the complete news.

87

President Harry S Truman announces to White House reporters the news of Japan's surrender.

American soldiers wave and cheer on their return to New York from Europe aboard the Queen Elizabeth.

ing reporters, they cheered.

Through the evening and into the night, Americans celebrated, wild with joy. City streets were jammed with throngs of laughing, shouting people. Men and women hugged one another; there were no strangers. Automobile horns blared and church bells rang. Special services of prayer and thanksgiving were held. In New York City, more than two million people poured into Times Square, where the cheering, embracing, and singing lasted until dawn.

On September 2, 1945, on the deck of the battleship *Missouri*, anchored in Tokyo Bay, the Allies and Japan signed the surrender agreement. General Douglas MacArthur signed on behalf of the Allied powers, and Admiral Chester Nimitz for the United States.

The war was finally over, but the price paid was high. This simple monument to a dead American soldier was created by his comrades, who used his fighting equipment to honor his sacrifice on the shell-blasted beaches of Normandy.

So ended the most brutal and destructive war in history. It killed more people and destroyed more property than any other war.

During the six years the war raged, more than 50 million people lost their lives. Of these about two thirds were civilians.

One can only estimate what the war cost in terms of property damage. Many of the major cities of the world lay in ruins. Millions of Europeans and Asians were starving and homeless.

For tens of millions who survived, the war held only tragic memories. "It is over — but not for all," wrote Hanson Baldwin in *The New York Times*. "Not for the maimed, the wounded, and the ill, not for those who hold within their hearts the sorrow unending. For them, the war goes on for years to come."

President Roosevelt (center), British Prime Minister Winston Churchill (left), and Generalissimo Joseph Stalin (right), of the Soviet Union, at the Lavadia Palace in Yalta.

Keeping the Peace

The United States and the other Allied nations accomplished what they set out to accomplish in World War II. They halted the aggression of Germany and Japan and stripped them of their military power.

But World War II created new problems. Keeping the peace was one of them.

In February 1945, about six months before the war ended, the leaders of the Big Three nations — Franklin Roosevelt, Winston Churchill, and Joseph Stalin — held a summit meeting at Yalta, a Soviet City on the Black Sea. There they settled military strategy for ending the war and attempted to solve the problems of a postwar Europe.

Edward R. Stettinius, Jr., Secretary of State and chairman of the United States delegation to the United Nations Conference, signs the United Nations charter on behalf of the United States government. President Harry S Truman stands at left.

The leaders agreed to divide Germany into four zones to be occupied by the United States, Great Britain, the Soviet Union, and France.

They also agreed to back a Soviet-supported government in Poland, where the Soviet Union promised to hold free elections.

In addition, the Soviet Union promised to enter the war against Japan. For this, the Soviets were awarded Japan's Kurile Islands and the northern half of Sakhalin Island.

Soviet leader Joseph Stalin kept only part of the bargain. Months later, on August 8, 1945, only six days before Japan surrendered, the Soviet Union finally declared war on Japan.

At Yalta, the three leaders had also agreed on a conference to prepare the United Nations charter. The charter was signed at San Francisco on June 26, 1945, by delegates of 50 nations. On October 24, 1945, the charter came into force, breathing life into an international effort to achieve lasting peace.

Memorable Dates, 1933–1946

1933

- Hitler comes to power as head of the Nazi Party.

1938

- Hitler invades Austria.
- Munich Pact signed between Great Britain, Germany, France, and Italy.
- Sudetenland in Czechoslovakia is given to Germany.

1939

- Remainder of Czechoslovakia taken by Germany.
- Poland invaded by Germany and later by Russia.
- Great Britain and France declare war on Germany.

1940

- Norway, Denmark, the Low Countries, and France invaded by Hitler.
- Dunkirk evacuation.
- Battle of Britain.

1941

- Japan attacks Pearl Harbor, Hawaii; also Guam and the Philippines.
- U.S. declares war on Japan.
- Germany and Italy declare war on the U.S.

1942

- First nuclear chain reaction is achieved.
- Rationing of gasoline, coffee, and other items begins.
- Battle of Stalingrad.
- Allied invasion of North Africa.

1943

- Allied forces invade Italy.
- Italy surrenders.

1944

- Allied forces land in France to liberate Europe.
- Franklin Roosevelt elected to fourth term.
- Battle of the Bulge.

1945

- Churchill, Stalin, and Roosevelt meet at Yalta Conference in Crimea, USSR.
- Franklin Roosevelt dies; Harry Truman becomes 33rd President.
- Germany surrenders.
- Atomic bombs dropped on Hiroshima and Nagasaki, Japan.
- Japan surrenders.
- Charter of the United Nations signed in San Francisco.

1946

- U.S. grants independence to Philippine Islands.
- UN headquarters established in New York City.

For Further Reading

Young Readers

Bliven, Bruce. *From Pearl Harbor to Okinawa: The War in the Pacific, 1941–1945.* New York: Random House, 1960.

Bliven, Bruce. *The Story of D-Day, June 6, 1944.* New York: Random House, 1963.

Claypool, Jane. *Hiroshima and Nagasaki.* New York: Franklin Watts, 1984.

Frank, Benis M. *Okinawa: The Great Island Battle.* New York: Talisman, Parrish Books, 1978.

Hough, Richard. *The Battle of Midway: Victory in the Pacific.* New York: The Macmillan Co., 1970.

Hoyt, Edwin P. *In the Deep: Pacific Submarine Action in World War II.* New York: G. P. Putnam's, 1978.

Lawson, Don. *An Album of World War II Home Fronts.* New York: Franklin Watts, 1980.

Lord, Walter. *The Miracle of Dunkirk.* New York: The Viking Press, 1982.

McKay, Ernest A. *Carrier Strike Force.* New York: Julian Messner Co., 1982.

McKay, Ernest A. *Undersea Terror: U-Boat Wolf Packs in World War II.* New York: Julian Messner Co., 1982.

Marrin, Albert. *Overlord, D-Day and the Invasion of Europe.* New York: Atheneum, 1983.

Marrin, Albert. *Victory in the Pacific.* New York: Atheneum, 1983.

Prager, Arthur, and Emily Prager. *World War II Resistance Stories.* New York: Franklin Watts, 1979.

Rossel, Seymour. *The Holocaust.* New York: Franklin Watts, 1981.

Young Adult Readers

Bailey, Richard H. *The Air War in Europe.* Alexandria, Virginia: Time-Life Books, 1949.

Baldwin, Hanson W. *Battles Lost and Won: Great Campaigns of World War II.* New York: Harper & Row, 1964.

Hersey, John. *Hiroshima.* New York: Alfred A. Knopf, 1978.

Liddell, Hart B. H. *History of the Second World War.* New York: G. P. Putnam's, 1970.

Lord, Walter. *Day of Infamy.* New York: Bantam Books, 1988.

Morison, Samuel Eliot. *The Two Ocean War: A Short History of the United States Navy in the Second World War.* Boston: Little, Brown & Co., 1963.

Parish, Thomas, ed. *The Simon & Schuster Encyclopedia of World War II.* New York: Simon & Schuster, 1978.

Prange, Gordon W. *At Dawn We Slept: The Untold Story of Pearl Harbor.* New York: McGraw-Hill Book Co., 1981.

Sears, Stephen W. *Desert War in North Africa.* New York: American Heritage Publishing Co., 1967.

Stokesbury, James L. *A Short History of World War II.* New York: William Morrow & Co., 1980.

Toland, John. *The Battle of the Bulge.* New York: Random House, 1966.

Index

Page references in italics indicate material in illustrations or photographs.

A

Aalborg, Denmark, *17*
Africa, battle for (Operation Torch), 44, *44*, 45, *45*
African Americans, war effort of, *49*, *51*, 53
Aircraft carriers, *5*. *See also* Naval power
    Japanese mainland raid and, 33–35
    Pearl Harbor raid and, 9
Air power
    African Americans, *49*, *51*
    Battle of Britain, 22, *22*, 23, *23*, 24, 25, *25*
    Dunkirk retreat, 19
    German defeat, 64
    German industry, 50, *50*, 51, *51*
    Pacific war, *72*, 73–74, 77–78, 79, *79*
    Pearl Harbor raid, *9*
Albania, Italian aggression against, 13
Aleutian Islands, battle for, 35–37
Algeria, 45
Arizona (battleship), *6*, 8, *9*
Atlantic Conference and Charter, 28, *29*
Atomic bomb
    development of, 83, 85
    Hiroshima bombing, 82, *82*, 83, *83*, *84*, 85
    Nagasaki bombing, 86
Auschwitz concentration camp, 71
Australia, Japan threatens, 33
Austria, German invasion of, 14
Axis powers, war declared on U.S. by, 10–11. *See also*
    Germany; Italy; Japan

B

Bataan Death March, 32
Battle of Britain, 22, *22*, 23, *23*, 24, *24*, 25, *25*
Battle of the Bulge, 62, *62*, 63, *63*
Belgium, 21
    allied liberation of, 62
    German invasion of, 18, *21*
Bergen-Belsen concentration camp, 69–70
Blitzkrieg warfare
    on Soviet Union, 27
    on Western Europe, 16–17
Buchenwald concentration camp, 71
Bulgaria, liberation of, 65
Burma, 13, 32
Bush, George, 80–81, *81*
Bushido (Japanese military code), 39

C

Canada, 23
Chamberlain, Neville
    fall of, 17
    Munich Pact and, 15
Chenango (aircraft carrier), *45*
Children, war effort of, 52, *53*
China
    Japanese invasion of, 12, *12*, 13
    U.S. air raid on Japan and, 34
Churchill, Winston, 23, *29*, *90*
    becomes prime minister of U.K., 17
    Dunkirk retreat and, 19
    Hitler, Adolf and, 21
    Roosevelt, Franklin D. and, 28, *29*
    Yalta Conference and, 90
Concentration camps, *15*, 69, *69*, 70, *70*, 71, *71*
Congress, war declared by, 10–11
Corregidor, *31*
Czechoslovakia

German invasion of, *14*, 15, 16
    liberation of, 65

D

Dachau concentration camp, *70*, 71
Daladier, Édouard, Munich Pact and, 15
Daniel, Lieutenant General von, *43*
D-Day invasion, *57*, *58*, *59*, *60*, *61*, 89
Death. *See* Fatalities
Denmark, German invasion of, 17, *17*, 21, *21*
Dunkirk retreat, 18–19, *19*, 20
Dutch. *See* Netherlands
Dutch East Indies, Japan occupies, 32

E

Egypt, 44
Eisenhower, Dwight D., *44*, 57, *57*, 63, 67
England. *See* Great Britain
Enola Gay (aircraft), 82, *82*
Estonia, Soviet Union occupies, 26
Ethiopia, Italian aggression against, 13

F

Fatalities. *See also* Prisoners of war
    civilian
        German, allied air raids, 50–51
        holocaust, 70
        Japanese
            air war, 79
            atomic bombings, 83, 86
        U.S., Pearl Harbor raid, *8*
    military
        allied forces, D-Day invasion, 60, 61
        German, Eastern front, 43
        Japanese, air war, 77–78
        U.S.
            atomic bomb decision and, 85
            Bataan Death March, 32
            Japanese air raids, 34
            Okinawa battle, 81
            Pacific war, 73
            Pearl Harbor raid, 9
    totals, 89
Finland, Soviet Union invades, 26
France
    allied invasion of, 57, *57*, 58, *58*, *59*, 60, *60*, 61, *61*, 62
    Dunkirk retreat and, 19
    fall of, 20–21, *21*
    German invasion of, *20*, *21*
    Germany occupied by, 91
    Germany threatens, 17
    liberation of, *64*
    Munich Pact and, 15
    Norway and, 17
    Poland and, 16

G

Germany
    aggression by, 13–15, 16
    air power, and, 22–25
    air war against, 50, *50*, 51, *51*
    allied invasion of, 62–63, 64
    Battle of the Bulge and, 62–63
    D-Day invasion and, 57–61
    France and, 17, 20, *20*, 21, *21*
    Great Britain and, 21
    military power of, *13*

Munich Pact and, 15
naval losses by, 17
North Africa and (Operation Torch), 44–45
occupation of, 91
Soviet Union invaded by, 26, *26*, 27, *27*, *42*, *43*
Stalingrad Battle and, 42–43
submarine warfare and, 40–41
surrender of, 64, 65, *66*, 67, *67*
war declared on U.S. by, 10–11
Great Britain
air war on, 22, *22*, 23, *23*, 24, *24*, 25, *25*
Dunkirk retreat and, 18, 19, *19*, 20
Germany and, 21
Germany occupied by, 91
Italy invaded by, 46–49
Japanese aggression against, 13
Munich Pact and, 15
North Africa and (Operation Torch), 44–45
Norway and, 17
Poland and, 16
prisoners of war, *17*
United States and, 28–29
Guadalcanal, battle for, 38, 39, *39*
Guam, 30, 32, *38*

H

Hamburg, Germany, bombing of, 50–51
Hawaiian Islands, 33. *See also* Pearl Harbor
Hiroshima, Japan, 82, *82*, 83, *83*, 84, 85
Hitler, Adolf, *12*, 14, 17, *18*, 29, *51*
aggression by, 14–15, *17*
Churchill, Winston and, 21
holocaust and, 69–71
military mistakes by, 27
politics of, 14
Stalingrad Battle and, 43
suicide of, 65
Holland. *See* Netherlands
Holocaust, *15*, 69, *69*, 70, *70*, 71, *71*
Homma, Masa Haru, *31*
Hong Kong, Japan occupies, 32
Hornet (aircraft carrier), 33, *33*, 36
Hungary, liberation of, 65

I

Indochina, Japanese aggression against, 13
Industry, bombing of Germany and, *50*, 50–51, *51*
Isolationists
Roosevelt, Franklin D. criticized by, 29
United States and, 28–29
Italy
aggression by, 13
allied invasion of, 46, *46*, 47, *47*, 48, *48*, 49, *49*
France attacked by, 20
Munich Pact and, 15
North Africa and (Operation Torch), 45
war declared on U.S. by, 10–11
Iwo Jima, battle for, 79, 80, *80*, 81, *81*

J

Japan
aggression by, 12–13
atomic bombing of, 82, *82*, 83, *83*, 84, 85, *85*, 86
China invaded by, *12*
military codes of, 39
Pacific Ocean conquests of, 30–32, 33
Pearl Harbor bombed by, 5–9

Philippines invaded by, 30, *31*
Soviet Union and, 91
surrender of, *86*, 86–89, *88*
U.S. air raids on, 33, *33*, 34, *34*, 35, 74, *79*
U.S. air war against, 79
U.S. naval war against, 72–74
U.S. plans invasion of, 81
Japanese-Americans, internment of, 54, *54*, 55
Jews
deportation of, *15*
Hitler and, 14
Holocaust and, 69, *69*, 70, *70*, 71, *71*
Jodl, Alfred, 67

K

Kamikaze attacks, 77, *77*, 78, 81
Kennedy, John F., 9, 35
Kiryu (aircraft carrier), *5*
Kiska Island, Japanese capture, 36
Kobe, Japan, U.S. air raids on, 33–35, 79

L

Latvia, Soviet Union occupies, 26
Lend Lease Act, 28, *28*
Leyte Gulf battle, 76–77, 78
Lithuania
liberation of, 65
Soviet Union occupies, 26
London, England, air war on, *22*. *See also* Battle of Britain
Luxembourg, German invasion of, 18, 21, *21*

M

MacArthur, Douglas, *76*
Japanese surrender and, 88
leaves Philippines, 30, 32
returns to Philippines, 75–76
Maginot Line, 17
Malaya, Japanese aggression against, 13, 32
Manchuria, Japan seizes, 12
Manila, Philippines
Japan attacks, 30
Japanese bombing of, *78*
Mariana Islands, *72*, *73*, 74, *74*, 79
Merchant ships, 28–29, 79
Midway Island
battle for, 35, *35*, 36, *36*, 37, *37*, 38
Japan attacks, 30
Japan threatens, 33
Missouri (battleship), 88
Morocco, 45
Munich Pact, World War II and, 15
Mussolini, Benito, *15*, 29
Ethiopia invaded by, 13
fall of, 48
France attacked by, 20

N

Nagasaki, Japan, atomic bombing of, 86
Nagoya, Japan, U.S. air raids on, 33–35, 79
Native Americans, war effort of, *74*
Naval power. *See also* Aircraft carriers
aircraft carriers, 9, 33–35
merchant ships, 28–29, 79
Pacific war and, 73–74, 75–78, 79, 81
submarine warfare, 40, *40*, 41, *41*
United States and, 29
Nazi Party, 14

Netherlands (Holland), 21
    allied liberation of, 62
    German invasion of, 18, *21*
    Japanese aggression against, 13, 32
Nimitz, Chester, 88
North Africa, battle for (Operation Torch), 44, *44*, 45, *45*
Norway, German invasion of, 17, *17*, 18, 21, *21*

O

Oil resources. *See* Petroleum
Okinawa, invasion of, 79, 80–81
Oklahoma (battleship), 8, 9
Operation Overlord. *See* D-Day invasion
Operation Torch, North Africa, 44, *44*, 45, *45*
Osaka, Japan, U.S. air raids on, 79

P

Paris, France, liberation of, *64*
Patton, George S., *45*
Pearl Harbor
    raid, *5, 6, 7, 8, 9,* 12, 30
    U.S. response to, *9,* 11, 29, 52
Petroleum
    Japan and, 79
    oilfield bombings, 51
    oil resources, 44
    rationing and, 56, *56*
Philippines
    fall of, 32, 33
    Japanese invasion of, 30, *31*
    U.S. returns to, 75, *75,* 76, *76,* 77, *77,* 78, *78*
Poland
    German invasion of, 16–17, *21*
    liberation of, 65
    Soviet Union and, 91
Potsdam Conference (July 1945), 85
Prisoners of war. *See also* Fatalities
    American, *63*
    British, *17*
    German, *43,* 48
    Japanese treatment of, *31,* 32
    Operation Torch, and, 45

Q

Queen Elizabeth (ocean liner), *88*

R

Radar, Great Britain and, 23
Rationing, 55, *55,* 56
Refugees, *25*
Romania
    allied bombing of, *50*
    liberation of, 65
Roosevelt, Elliot, *29*
Roosevelt, Franklin D., *10, 29, 46, 90*
    Churchill, Winston and, 28, *29*
    death of, 65, *68,* 83
    isolationist attacks on, 29
    war declaration and, 10–11
    Yalta Conference and, 90
Russia. *See* Soviet Union

S

Saipan, Mariana Islands, *72, 73, 74*
Sicily
    allied invasion of, *46, 47*
    allies occupy, 46
    North African war and, 45
Siegfried Line, 17

Singapore, Japan attacks, 32
Smith, Walter Bedell, 67
Solomon Islands, battle for, 38–39
Soviet Union, 17
    Berlin falls to, 65, 67
    Eastern Europe liberated by, 64–65
    German invasion of, 26, *26,* 27, *27*
    Germany occupied by, 91
    Japan and, 91
    Lend Lease Act and, *28*
    Poland attacked by, 16
    Poland dominated by, 91
    Stalingrad defense, 42, *42,* 43, *43*
    United States and, 28, 65
Stalin, Joseph, 26, 27, 90, *90,* 91
Stalingrad, Soviet Union, defense of, 42, *42,* 43, *43*
Stettinius, Edward R., Jr., *91*
Submarine warfare
    Germany, 40, *40,* 41, *41*
    U.S., 79
Sudentenland, German invasion of, 15
Suez Canal, 44
Sutherland, Richard, *76*

T

Tibbets, Paul W., Jr., *82*
Tojo, Hideki, 12
Tokyo, Japan, U.S. air raids on, 33–35, 79, *79*
Truman, Harry S, 67, 86, *88, 91*
    assumes Presidency, 65
    atomic bomb and, 83, 85, 87
Tunisia, 45

U

U-boats. *See* Submarine warfare
United Nations, 28, 91, *91*
United States
    air war against Japan, 33, *33,* 34, *34,* 35, 79
    Germany occupied by, 91
    home front in, 52, *52,* 53, *53,* 54, *54,* 55, 56
    isolationist politics in, 28–29
    Italy invaded by, 46–49
    naval war against Japan, 72–74
    North Africa and (Operation Torch), 44–45
    Soviet Union and, 65
United States Congress, war declared by, 10–11

W

Wake Island, 30, *30,* 32
Women
    armed forces and, 11, *11*
    war effort of, 52, *52,* 53, *53,* 55
Women Accepted for Volunteer Emergency Service
    (WAVES), 11
Women's Army Corps (WACS), *10,* 11, *55*
World War I, 14, 20
World War II
    aftermath of, 90–91
    German aggression and, 13–15
    Germany surrenders, 64–67
    Holocaust and, 69–71
    Italian aggression and, 13
    Japanese aggression and, 12–13
    Japan surrenders, 86, *86,* 87, 88, *88,* 89
    U.S. enters, 10–11

Y

Yalta Conference, *90,* 90–91
Yorktown (aircraft carrier), *35,* 36, *37*